Essentially, Zurich and Basel no longer have any insoluble problems on their own urban territory. All Swiss cities have a problem of form outside the city core.

Marcel Meili

Looking from Wangen-Brüttisellen in the direction of Greifensee, around 1920

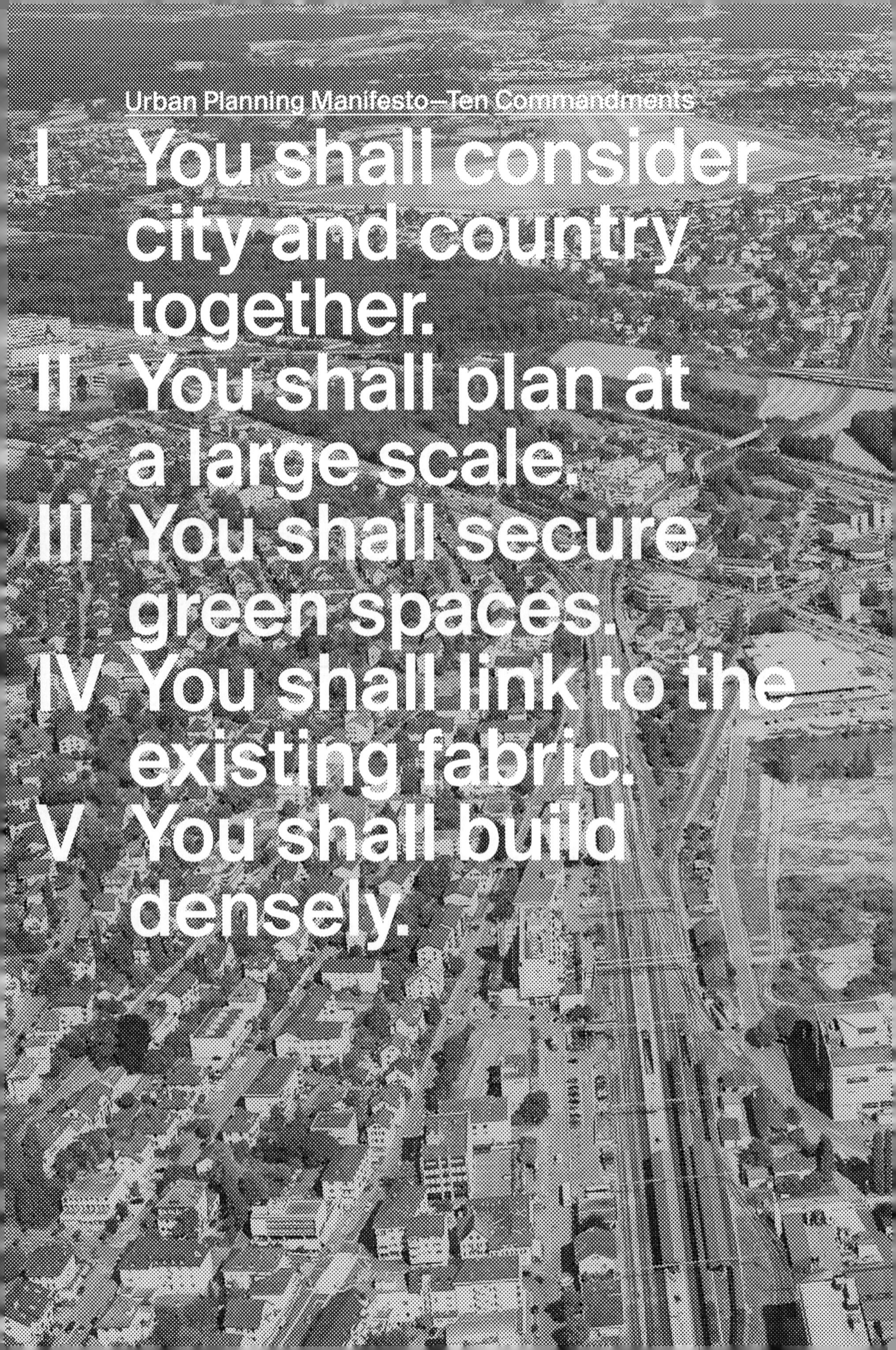

Urban Planning Manifesto—Ten Commandments

I You shall consider city and country together.

II You shall plan at a large scale.

III You shall secure green spaces.

IV You shall link to the existing fabric.

V You shall build densely.

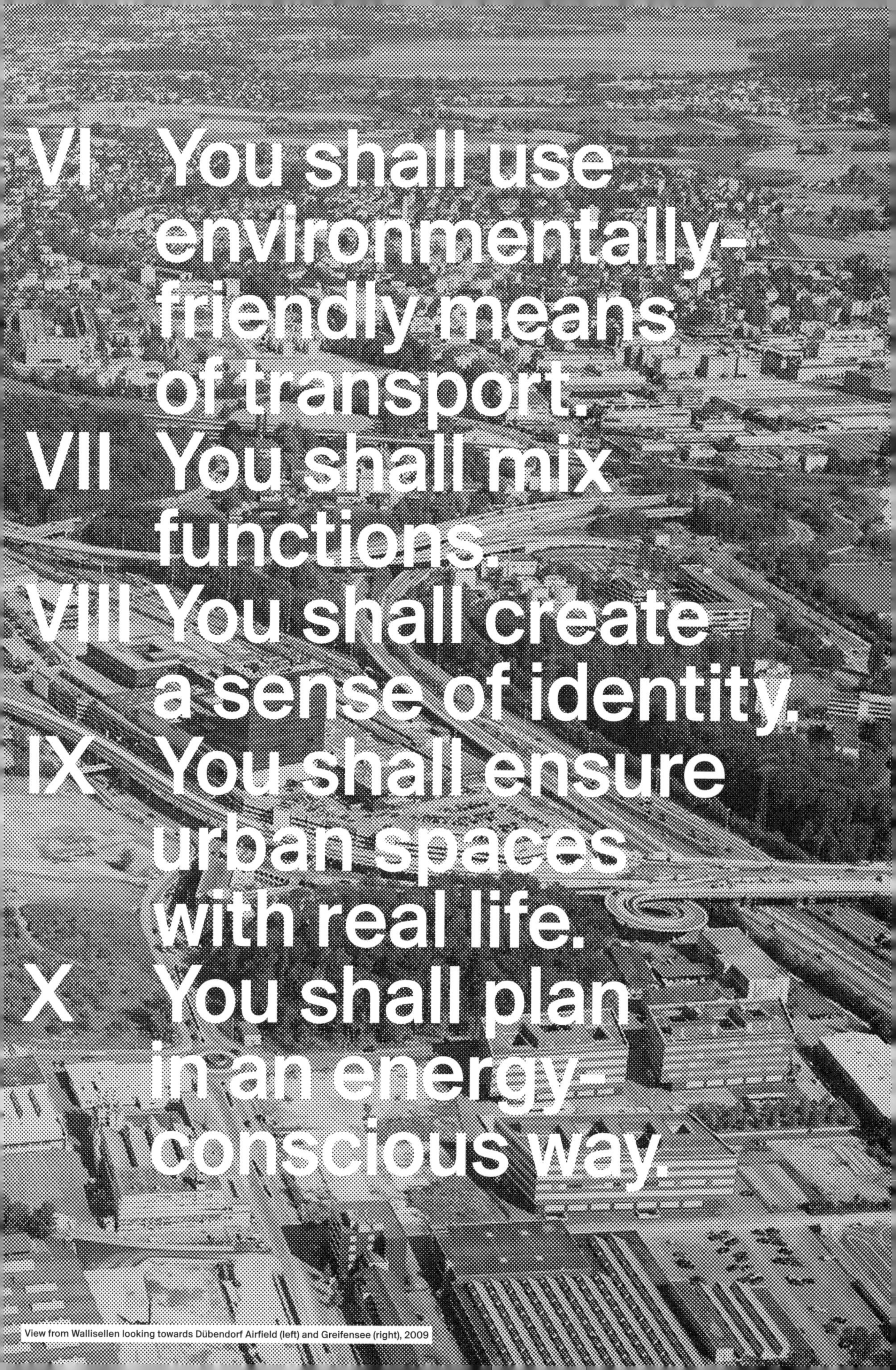

VI You shall use environmentally-friendly means of transport.

VII You shall mix functions.

VIII You shall create a sense of identity.

IX You shall ensure urban spaces with real life.

X You shall plan in an energy-conscious way.

View from Wallisellen looking towards Dübendorf Airfield (left) and Greifensee (right), 2009

Setup International Summer Academy Zurich

Architects Group Krokodil

1 North Coast
The development of a stable, spatial-strategic, and programmatic framework that will allow the affected communities to grow together gradually in a focused, high-quality way.

2 Motorway Park
Transformation of residual spaces, bridging the motorway with landscape bridges to create large-scale linking elements between districts. Development of new, dense (multi-story) commercial typologies within reach of residential districts.

3 Core Area Airfield
Development of lively urban districts that can be traversed on foot, which have a high density resulting from new, mixed-use typologies and concentrations of cultural and research uses that shape the character of the city.

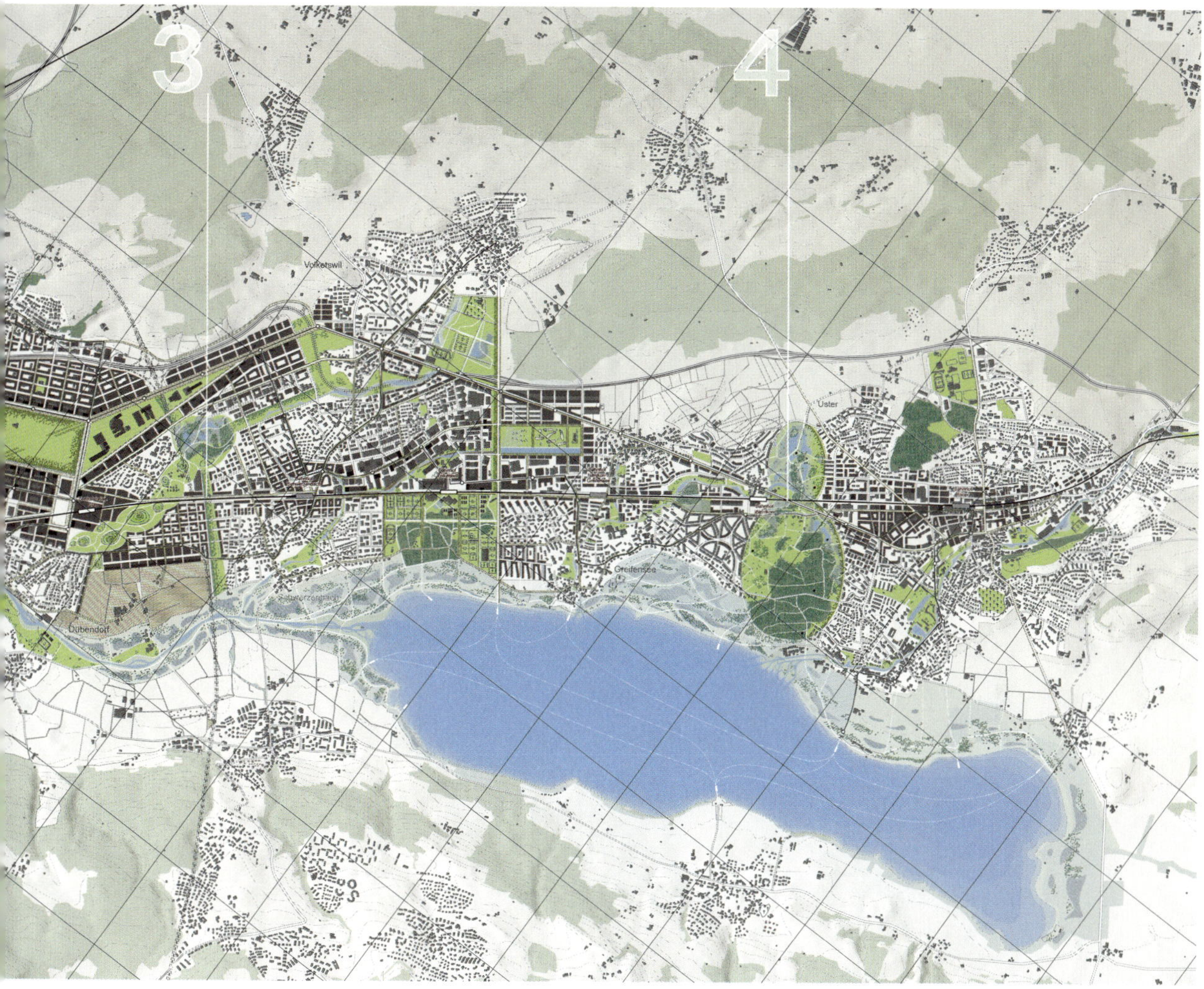

Overall plan: Glatt—the city, with four intervention areas

Intervention areas

The chosen areas of intervention are large and have been defined broadly. However, they all provide a different thematic accent in the overall idea of a diversified city. Each area covers different aspects of the city, and as many locations as possible. Depending on the briefs of individual studios, it is possible to focus on either more general connections or precise and in-depth study of a local area. The preceding study of the Glatttal can, but must not necessarily form the basis for the work. The overlap between areas already indicates that the spatial boundaries are blurred, that there exist no clear distinctions. Two studio groups have been allocated to each task.

4 Landscape Park

The potential of suburban settlements in high-quality landscape areas, with a focus on reactivating the existing outdoor space and connecting the surrounding communities to the landscape. Encouragement of dense residential forms for the benefit of the landscape.

Glatttal

An important guiding principle for the Glatttal city is the idea of a city with generous green space. One of the main ideas is an interconnected system of corridors, interspersed with pockets for leisure activities. These pockets vary in size, program, and atmosphere.

1m2/sec 08/15

Marc Angélil

Thank you for the invitation and introductory remarks. It is a great pleasure to participate in this symposium at the Summer Academy in Zurich. My intervention is entitled 1m2/sec 08/15. 1m2/sec stands for the speed of urbanization processes that are generally associated with what has been termed *urban sprawl*, a process using one square meter of land per second. 08/15, an idiom in colloquial German to describe run-of-the-mill phenomena, stands for the mediocre standards associated with urbanization processes. The norms are given and the mechanisms at work precisely determined. The formula 1m2/sec 08/15 addresses the *modus operandi* of contemporary urban production and combines the velocity of land consumption with generally agreed upon standards. What follows below are a few observations on the formation of current urban territories.

First observation: We are shooting with gunfire at the territory—possibly in analogy to a technique used by Marcel Duchamp in his work *The Bride Stripped Bare by Her Bachelors, Even*, known as *The Large Glass*. ↗ Fig. 1 Duchamp's art piece was created over a long period of time, from 1915 to 1923, and could be read as a snapshot of a process, with time momentarily standing still. The work could be considered unfinished. As with a palimpsest, one encounters here a process of layering. Duchamp added one layer on top of the other. Occasionally, some parts were erased to add another layer. While doing so, he experimented with different techniques, which left their marks—as deposits—within the space of the painting. When, for example, the glass pane broke during transport, the cracks were accepted as part of the work. One technique, in particular, shall be foregrounded: just below the cloud, on the top right corner of the glass, one detects a zone with dots. These are the shots of the nine bachelors. Duchamp used a toy gun and matches dipped in paint as ammunition to create a representation of bullet holes on the painting's surface.

1 Marcel Duchamp, *The Bride Stripped Bare by Her Bachelors, Even (The Large Glass)*, 1915–1923

Second observation: A children's book by the illustrator Jörg Müller entitled *Alle Jahre wieder saust der Presslufthammer nieder* offers another take on the matter. ↗ Fig. 2 The book was published in 1973 and subsequently translated into several languages, including French, English, and Chinese. Expressions such as *Die Veränderung der Landschaft, La mutation d'un paysage*, or *Changing Countryside* point to the very transformation of territory—from a more or less rural state to what we might call today an urban landscape that is neither rural nor urban.

2 Jörg Müller, *Alle Jahre wieder saust der Presslufthammer nieder oder die Veränderung der Landschaft*, 1962

The book consists of seven panels each covering a period of three years and depicting, through a type of time lapse technique, the conversion of a specific place starting at a specific moment in time: the village of Güllen in May 1953. ↗ Fig. 3

1956: signs of a transformation are barely visible, for *change* is only slowly creeping in. A street is widened and covered with asphalt, a creek straightened and canalized in concrete pipes. 1959: the idyllic atmosphere seems to be still intact. Upon closer look, one discerns what a few changes and erasures of the existing entail, without leaving any traces of time: a farm is demolished, a forest cleared. 1963: the frequency of interventions accelerates, that is, the number of recurring events per time unit. The forest has been replaced by large tanks and the farm by a factory building. ↗ Fig. 4 1966: The autonomy of each event evades any possibility of coordination. One never really knows what might happen next, when and where: a high-rise building is built in Güllen; the old railroad crossing at grade is replaced by an underpass; a suburban development with cookie-cutter houses emerges outside the village. 1969: despite the fact that every intervention is meticulously planned down to the last detail, the resulting urban entity nonetheless looks like an accidental assembly of isolated incidences. A street is relocated, the underpass widened, a new church built. 1972: nothing is left to chance. Every intervention follows clearly established and generally accepted norms and protocols, applied again and again—standard 08/15 family houses, normative 08/15 freeways, typical 08/15 shopping malls, and so on … ↗ Fig. 5

3 6 May 1953

4 19 January 1963

5 3 October 1972

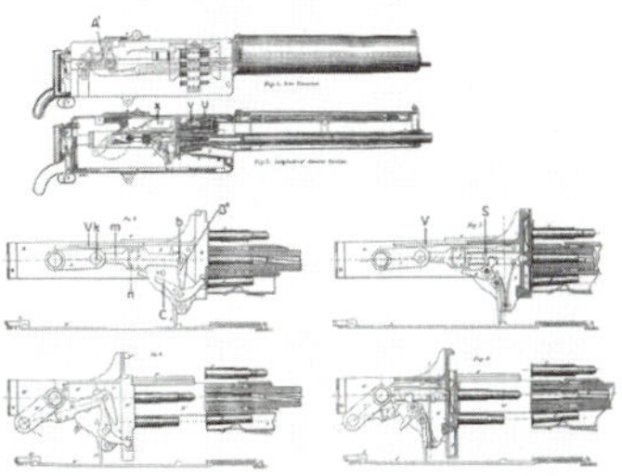

6 Hiram Stevens Maxim, patent drawing of the machine gun 08/15, 1888

DIN

7 Deutsche Industrie Norm (DIN)

Third observation: Few know that 08/15 was originally the designation of a machine gun of the German infantry during World War I. ↗ Fig. 6 The model with the serial number 08/15 stood for a new system of industrial production, a system requiring well-tuned coordination between the public and private sector. The institutional network that was established had all the characteristics of a machine, or *megamachine* to use an expression coined by Lewis Mumford. Megamachines are organizations put in place to achieve a specific purpose—in our case, the making of an automatic weapon. They require an efficient bureaucratic apparatus. Minute changes within the system set a chain of administrative procedures in motion. Most importantly, assemblies of this type tend to take on a life of their own.

The machine gun was made up of a series of parts that were manufactured in different factories. In addition to State agencies and university laboratories, more than 100 firms were involved in the production of the weapon. In order to facilitate communication, specific norms had to be established, including uniform measuring techniques, standardized templates, material specifications, and agreed upon tolerances. The definition of such guidelines ultimately led to the establishment of the German Institute for Standardization, the *Deutsches Institut für Normung* (DIN). ↗ Fig. 7

The machine gun is made up of components that are added to one another to form a closed system (1+2+3+4+5). Each part performs a limited number of binary functions: open-closed, on-off, engaged-disengaged (0-1-0-1-0). The individual components are produced in series and are entirely identical (1/1/1/1/1). ↗ Fig. 8 In other words, the addition of precision parts, the performance of predetermined functions, and the logic of mass production are key characteristics of the machine gun 08/15.

Efficiency, combined with the logic of rational thought, is at the core of the development. The objective is to maintain control. Complex technical requirements and organizational effectiveness are merged to achieve order, or to use a term from system theory, to build up negentropy. However, the norm was not as perfect as originally planned. The machine gun had its problems and was soon discredited by the soldiers as flawed and uninspired, which explains the current use of the term 08/15 as denoting something bland and banal. But that is not all: the deployment of the weapon on the battlefield led to the exact opposite of order, exposing the dark side of the war machinery. The gun was named *L'arrosoir du diable*—the devils watering-can. At the front, in the battle zones, instead of order, a high degree of entropy arose.

Fourth observation: The photograph *The Bridge* by Jeff Wall shows a typical condition encountered nowadays at the edges of cities, a trivial space that demarks the dullness of everyday life in contemporary suburban territories—the physical manifestation of what could be called a form of 08/15 urbanism. ↗ Fig. 9 Urbanization entails the deployment of normed products. The urban fabric is made up of components that can be applied again and again in different situations. The development of each element follows precisely determined norms that manifest themselves in prototypical forms. These are genetically ingrained in local zoning plans and ordinances. And so, one encounters today always much the same kind of housing and retail developments, with similar densities, identical setbacks, and given typologies. The colorful appearance of zoning plans is deceptive. Instead of differentiation: a featureless substance framing the reality of contemporary agglomerations. ↗ Fig. 10

Rotaries, for example, are typical elements of the contemporary urban fabric. They are hailed by traffic engineers and municipal authorities as unprecedented in their efficacy—wonder machines far surpassing the performance of traditional street junctions. A near endless number of manuals and regulations clearly outline when and where to use rotaries. The norms are given. And so it is that the city is formed, according to a body of objectively justified rules that regulate collectively adopted practices, which are endorsed—in the case of the rotaries—by the public hand.

The private sector operates according to similar procedures. Here as well, norm rules. A deep-rooted mentality, driven by rationally justified efficiency, guides all operations, as in the case of the big box discount stores, which have literally taken the urban periphery by storm. "Make it simple" is the motto of this industry. The number of procedural steps is kept to a minimum and the logistical protocols are standard issue. They determine, as blueprints, the siting of buildings, their size, organization, construction, and the make-up of their interior spaces.

Fifth observation: If the land is the target, then the ammunition comprises standardized type forms, which are, literally, shot at territory, as depicted in an aerial photograph of a recently developed tract of land in the State of Arkansas, in the so-called Fayetteville-Springdale-Rogers Metropolitan Statistical Area—the official designation of this region. ↗ Fig. 11 A patch of city or a piece of conurbation that sprung from the ground within just a few years through additive, step by step procedures—the principle of and, and, and. In chronological order: the Interstate 540 with two exits and their typical on- and off-ramps; a private hospital; the Mercy Medical Center; a Walmart store in close proximity to a planned and never realized suburban neighborhood; a business park for the regional branch of Morgan Stanley Smith Barney; a megachurch; a hotel with conference and convention center; a Target department store; the shopping center Pinnacle Hills Promenade. ↗ Fig. 12

All components follow standardized rules. One always knows exactly what and how to build: Samples taken from the fabric of the contemporary urban landscape point to the consequences of such processes.

On the one hand, territorial development is controlled by rules aimed at establishing order. On the other hand, this order cannot be found. Quite the

1 + 2 + 3 + 4 + 5

0 - 0 - 0 - 0 - 0

1 / 1 / 1 / 1 / 1

8 Characteristics of assembly, performance, and production: the principle of addition, binary functions, and serial fabrication

9 Jeff Wall, *The Bridge*, 1980

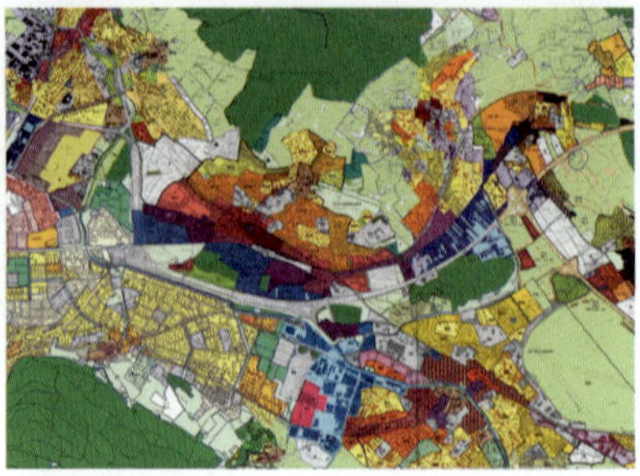

10 Montage of zoning plans of the Zurich region, 2004

opposite, the greater the claim for order, the more disorder is encountered. Notwithstanding all planning efforts, the city eludes orderly measures. Inherent to the urban aggregate is the tendency to progressively increase its entropy. Whereas each intervention is logically justified, the territory seems more and more to display the characteristics of a battle field.

What we come across here is a strange reversal of phenomena: order lapses into disorder, negentropy into entropy. The rationality of procedures leads to irrational assemblages.

This undercuts the principles propagated by traditional urban discourse, undermining its biases in favor of logically deduced objectives. Those convoluted mechanisms that likewise regulate the conditions of the 1m2/sec 08/15 city are beyond its field of vision.

Sixth and seventh observation: Let us dig deeper into the subject matter: the following observations address space and time and their design potentials **Concerning space, the proposition: Form instead of Norm. 08/15 urbanism must be radically transformed ... away from its anonymous conformity ... towards the specific form-gestalt of space.** Concerning time, the proposition of its rediscovery: instead of the rate of consumption 1m2/sec, an entirely different way of conceptualizing time in territory.

Initially, three colors shall be distinguished to address the territorial organization of large agglomerations: red, black, and green—*le rouge, le noir, et le vert*. The colors represent different subsystems of the urban landscape. Red stands for the built fabric, black for infrastructure, and green, as one would expect, for landscape. ↗ Fig. 13 Red, in its tendency to sprawl, always displaces green. Black calls the shots, insofar as development always follows the lines in black. Green as background and hinterland is permanently on the defensive. We encounter here a kind of machine, a *ménage à trois* of unequal players. These must be brought, according to the recently published *Spatial Concept Switzerland*, into a new and more balanced relationship. The demands are bold in their potential consequences. Red must be tamed: *contain sprawl—do not encroach on landscape—densify the fabric and increase functional interaction*. In short: no additional red patches. Black must be sparsely applied: *contain mobility—maintain existing networks—increase capacity without additional infrastructure*. In short: no additional black lines. Green as the weaker partner must be protected: *"contain land use—maintain the landscape as resource—promote agriculture and safeguard biodiversity."* In short: do not touch green.With this, a great deal could be achieved for the quality of space at the territorial level.

But let us add a few additional colors, possibly in reference to Andy Warhol's *Paint by Numbers series*. ↗ Fig. 14 Here, the colors could represent spatial attributes, atmospheres, images, i.e., properties that qualify space. We are talking here about the identification-potential *of*

11 "Seewenmarkt," Schwyz, 2007

12 The Fayetteville-Springdale-Rogers Metropolitan Statistical Area, Arkansas

Le Rouge et le Noir et le Vert

13 Alluding to Stendhal's novel *Le rouge et le noir*, colors are used to identify the subsystems of the urban terrain

space, made possible by characteristics inscribed in territory. Take, for example, the region of Zurich, and subdivide it according to the paint by numbers method into districts, neighborhoods, or boroughs with distinctive traits, as suggested by berchtoldkrass for the Metropolitan Conference Zurich. ↗ Fig. 15 What would emerge is an intriguing mosaic, rather than a zoning plan, something closer to an identification-map registering not quantities *per se* but formative qualities.

Each metro-neighborhood has site-specific characteristics. These need to be recognized and their differences fostered. A kind of butterfly collection would arise. Rather than encouraging monocultures, the city would be formed by a diversity of species. The reading of space is framed here by visually perceived distinctions, as put forth by Vittorio Lampugnani's *Manual on the Periphery*. Critical herein is the ease with which particular spatial elements can be discerned and the ability to combine them to form comprehensive image-patterns. The design of recognizable elements is thus a precondition for a collective appropriation of space. Thus far, observations on space: These must be broadened to include the element of time, as space always comprises a temporal dimension. **Urbanity, as we know, encompasses the production of space in time, or to be more specific, the creation of organized space-time relations.** Called for is a rediscovery of time in space. A sketch by Paul Hofer illustrates the issue. Superimposed onto the plan of a pedestrian underpass at the Bern train station are the fortifications of the city dating from the fourteenth and fifteenth centuries—a type of double exposure of different moments in time. **André Corboz, in his essay "The Land as Palimpsest," correspondingly describes the city as a process in which parts are successively erased and added. A key characteristic of a palimpsest is its transformation: per definition, palimpsests are manuscripts from which the text has been scraped off in order to be re-used again.** Corboz appropriates this concept to describe transformation processes encountered in cities, as shown, for example, by Aldo Rossi's analysis of the city of Split. The urban fabric is read as a form of writing modified by time. While some elements and structures change, others remain; for example, those of the Palace of Diocletian, which are literally inscribed within the urban text. ↗ Fig. 16 **"Every territory," writes Corboz, "exists only once. ... It must therefore continually be reclaimed."** An installation, for instance, by a Boston group of architects and artists—appropriately entitled *Drawing on Site: Pathways for Reclamation*—depicts different time-layers physically engraved in space.

Urban structures are written by means of cartographic notations transposed onto the territory. However, this process is not unified, but is marked by ruptures, a-temporalities, conflicts, and contradictions.

14 Andy Warhol, *Do It Yourself* (Landscape), 1962

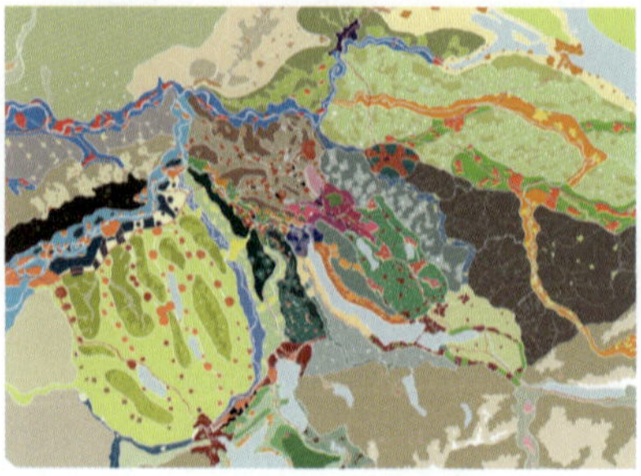

15 Identification map that registers formative characteristics of the urban landscape, 2011

16 Illustration from Vittorio Magnago Lampugnani's and Matthias Noell's publication *Handbuch zum Stadtrand*, 2007

Notwithstanding the notion of the city as an entity, as generally promoted within the history of architecture, the city has always been a conglomerate composed of fragments—a palimpsest resulting from a space-time stratification, whether by subtraction or addition.

Such accumulation processes have design potential. Instead of *tabula rasa* as exclusive planning principle, one could consider the possibility of inscribing time in space. Temporality within our discipline has visual properties as well. One not only reads space *per se*, but space in relation to time. The city fabric is formed by space-time compressions.

We are talking here about a literal densification ... a densification not only of the built fabric ... not exclusively of functional relations ... but most importantly, a densification of time, with identity-forming potential.

And it is in this sense that one could continue to work, in order to tackle the contemporary urban landscape, not only as a phenomenon, but as a possible design endeavor. To paraphrase Robert Musil: in order to transform what could be termed "a city without qualities" into "a city with qualities."

Text based on lecture delivered on July 26, 2012 at the International Summer Academy Zurich

Retrofitting Suburbia

Freek Persyn

Persyn 51N4E 060 OCMW-Nevele

The claim that we need to go from suburb to city can easily be misleading, as it can prevent us from focusing on the real problem at hand. It suggests a paradigmatic shift, leaving a suburban model behind and trying to realize an urban model instead. By trying to achieve a clear condition—where city is city and countryside is countryside—one might end up in a hopeless quest for a strict separation between supposedly clear categories. Accepting the fact that such a distinction does not really exist in the first place, we believe it is more strategically sensible to look at how built and open space can interact. This attitude will allow the invention of a series of productive relations on a variety of scales, from the regional to the architectural. To imagine new possibilities of this kind is a challenge of the utmost importance and meeting it should enable us to use these possibilities for both the development of new city parts and the retrofit of the suburban environments left to us by the previous century.

Text based on lecture delivered on July 24, 2012 at the International Summer Academy Zurich

Typology Transfer

Emanuel Christ & Christoph Gantenbein

Still from the film *Remaking Zurich* by ETH-Studio Emanuel Christ and Christoph Gantenbein

In making a collage, things come together that initially have nothing to do with one another. Therein lies the potential of collage. When collaging, unexpected issues arise and surprising insights come about with respect to one's own project. As a byproduct, the design process also becomes a learning process. While designing and manipulating the building types, we truly learn their attributes and potentials. It definitely gets exciting when we realize the transfer has left its mark on the transferred type—because a building type is not stable; it is subject to constant changes. This instability—the potential for further development—is what we want to sound out and harness when we insert building types into a new context. Our hope lies in the potential for change.

Text based on lecture delivered on July 24, 2012 at the International Summer Academy Zurich

Incremental Masterplanning

Angelus Eisinger

The idea of the master plan is accompanied by the confidence of order. Its logic is based on the principle of complete and visually powerful composition, which has guided ideas on urban planning since the mid-nineteenth century. The master plan promises the systematic organization of entire cities or urban districts to subsequently elaborate the elements of this order, and ultimately implement them, plot by plot, ensemble by ensemble—always according to the concept of the major overriding idea. But in the urbanized landscapes of the current *condition urbaine* there are few points at which this idea can be applied.

In Switzerland, in particular, as Marcel Meili emphasizes, the small-scale nature of the conditions hinders focused work at the dimensions of a master plan. According to Martin Heller, this fragmentation and its enormous political inertia should not, however, be mistaken for diversity. Whereas the former blocks the reshaping of space, the latter relates to the complexity of identities, patterns of perception, and forms of appropriation of the actual territory.

Here lies the decisive starting point for a focused transformation that goes beyond the plot—that is, beyond the realm of the architectural object and urban planning ensemble. In the process, the task for architects who plan the city is radically altered as compared to working on the classic master plan. The central challenge, as Alexandre Chemetoff makes clear, is to determine from the nature of the concrete project, which program is relevant to the specific place—i.e., specifying abstract concepts such as density, materiality, or public nature out of and with the contexts in which the urban project then unfolds its physical presence and everyday impact. A step-by-step approach is made to what Chemetoff calls "reinvention of the program"—concrete, precise, relevant to architecture and everyday life beyond the perimeter of the intervention.

A plan of this kind, based on carefully considered interventions, mediates between apparently contradictory logics. It transports and condenses an image of everyday urban life in a state of change, which establishes binding orientation without anticipating the future. It sees itself as the momentum of a permanent transformation of the existing on its path to a new order and its appropriation in everyday life. An approach of this kind relies on key projects and small areas of intervention (Roger Diener), which together redirect the vectors of spatial development beyond their spatial boundaries. Aesthetics and the question of design acquire a central role here: according to Chemetoff, it is intervention become architecture that changes people's perception and consequently also their understanding of places and spaces. In these shifts, new urban images anchor themselves and new conditions in the scale of the city crystallize.

Conversion of the printing works in the old armaments factory into a kindergarten and public spaces, Saint-Etienne, 2009/2013

The ships of the Loire: refurbishment and conversion of four industrial sheds, Ile-de-Nantes, 2005/2007

Text based on panel delivered on July 24, 2012 at the International Summer Academy Zurich

Just Imagine a City Is Made and No One Shows up There

Andreas Ruby

A better urban expansion area than the one in Neu-Oerlikon probably cannot be built. The architecture is of a high quality, the public spaces are decently sized, and the materials used for the urban user interfaces were chosen with great care. There is no shortage of bike paths, playgrounds for children, parks for adults, and even a certain number of public amenities and shops. In fact, everything seems to have been thought of. And yet it is not really urban. It is a summer day, the weather is wonderful and yet there are hardly any people around. A palpable air of boredom wafts invisibly through the well-defined outdoor space that gives the impression of something that was once ordered but never collected. The features that do exist point out, with an almost painful clarity, what could be here, but is nowhere to be found: people, actions, shouts, smells, hordes of children that leave turmoil in their wake. A kingdom for a hint of chaos that might disturb the stolid composure of this leaden order. But at Max-Bill-Platz one will wait in vain for Lautréamont's "chance meeting on a dissecting table between a sewing machine and an umbrella," which the Surrealists regarded as an ontological X-ray of modern society. This space is the guarantee, poured in concrete, of its designed lack of incident. An esoteric monument to the notion that it is possible to build the city. Most architects believe this, too—otherwise, why bother with urban planning? But: one can only plan and build the body of the city, not the life that makes it pulsate. If, according to Berkeley, something exists only when it is perceived (*esse est percipi*), then the city first exists when it has been appropriated. The malaise of the New Swiss Suburb is a consequence of its failure to be appropriated. And this appropriation does not take place partly because the planned city conveys exactly the opposite. The virtuoso over-design that drips from every pore is no more than a three-dimensionally coded behavioral manual to inhibit individuals' interactions: don't paint anything here, murmur the immaculate surfaces. Don't put anything there, warn the neatly defined open spaces. And for goodness sake don't get in the way, hisses the smart-ass circulation system. If a system is perfect, then all that human beings do is upset it. In this sense, the absence of spatial appropriation in the New Swiss Suburb is a consequence of the exaggerated presence of architecture and its leaden fetish of "quality." Gradually, it is beginning to dawn on a few people that the quasi fundamentalist cult of the architectural actually prevents the city from developing its "cityness" (Saskia Sassen). Many cities that fascinate us from an urban point of view are architecturally mediocre but compensate for this apparent deficiency by an overwhelming culture of the public realm: street food, street art, all kinds of improvised programs that respond to urban desires rather than disciplining them and all of this takes place in a permanent, beguiling osmosis between the inside and outside world of the city. In these adrenalin-impregnated spheres of urbanity, plans are, as a rule, made to be later ignored or discarded if necessary. On the day when the same can be said of the New Swiss Suburb, the agglomeration will experience its Armageddon and the city its hallelujah.

Shopping Center "Espiral", Quito, Ecuador

UNAM (Universidad Nacional Autonoma de Mexico), Mexico-City

Text based on panel delivered on July 30, 2012 at the International Summer Academy Zurich

Identity Markers. The Question of Authoring Space in Post-Fordism

André Bideau

The recent growth of the city of Zurich occurred with little or no theoretical underpinning, largely beyond the focus of public attention and debate. It can best be described as a learning-by-doing experience, a shift in methodology that forced personnel, designers, and the entire institutional framework to respond to drastic economic changes, while a new rapport arose between capital, program, infrastructure, and place. Confronted with a textbook case of deindustrialization, there was practically no broader conversation on what the city of Zurich should be about, and in those cases where there was one, negotiations were typically shielded from the public sphere. The real estate interests at stake primarily concerned the private sector. A side effect of the growing intimacy of real estate and local governance in Zurich and elsewhere, the issue of identity has gained an increasingly central role in urban development.

A spectacular example of this paradigm shift can be found in the immediate vicinity of the 2012 Summer Academy venue: the formal master plan for the industrial zones of Oerlikon. Here one sees the built results of ambitious real estate goals that were set twenty years ago. This industrial redevelopment site, the largest in Switzerland, became a showcase for planning and also the image of the institutional and economic framework in its time—now already recent history. The challenge of creating a new urban identity on a vast scale was met with a fairly rigid plan. With their design, Silva Ruoss, Karen Schrader, and Cary Siress cast an image for an entire neighborhood that would occupy a previously forbidden city of machine industry. The 1992 plan took the former manufacturing buildings as inspiration for a vast continuous space, emulating a monumental industrial scale, yet with little use for the fragments left behind. Camillo Sitte was revisited with a fabric of interlocking spaces and uniform building heights featuring formalized pockets of landscape architecture. Today, the clear-cut blocks of an almost anonymous architecture offer their commentary on the fabric of post-industrial Zurich.

The holistic approach of the Oerlikon plan proved problematic during the ensuing 1990s recession when an incremental approach to accommodate shifts in programming would have proven more versatile. Through zoning decisions, the extensive master plan had dictated an even split of one-third housing, one-third office use, and one-third industrial manufacturing. ↗ Fig. 1 Like with the formally sophisticated design, the municipal authorities had been able to impose the rigidity of usage upon the two landowners. In exchange for this concession, real estate development was granted a *tabula rasa* that left practically nothing of the former factory buildings. Ironically, the new industrial facilities erected by ABB, the main landowner, quickly became underutilized shells as manufacturing dwindled and was relocated to the ABB plant in Baden.

1 Postindustrial Oerlikon: housing morphology on redeveloped site

2 Former MFO factory building from 1876, now "Branding House" headquarters, during 2012 relocation

The sparse remnants of Oerlikon's historic past were subjected to a process of fastidious remanufacturing. Insignificant, but highly visible within the first tier of new construction, an ancillary building was shifted to a new location when the Swiss railway required additional space for new track in 2012. ↗ Fig. 2 The nineteenth-century brick structure now has the character of an industrial fetish. Its current tenant is the consulting firm *Branding House*, further underscoring the role of identity fabrication in the post-industrial present. It is telling that the challenges to Zurich's self-definition arose after the S-Bahn (commuter railway) was inaugurated in 1990. Although fundamentally altering relationships in the Zurich metropolitan region with a new level of mobility, the rail network was designed with neither an urban nor a regional planning strategy. Little attention was paid to the role the S-Bahn nodes would play for the western and northern city edges—areas where the deindustrialization process had already begun. Navigating north of Oerlikon today, little homogeneity can be seen, not to speak of attempts to formally address public space. Instead, one encounters a slew of infrastructural and technological fragments, mixed in with a multitude of building scales, a blend that is at times vigorous, at times depressingly generic. This landscape testifies to a bygone era in which areas, such as that now known as Glatttal city, were disposable zones where the necessities of contemporary consumer society could be located, a programming reinforced by the anaesthetization of Zurich's historic center.

Another layer contaminates and blends in with the fragmented texture of Glatttal city, in turn spawning programs on a novel scale: Parts of the zone belong to the service corridor that spans from downtown Zurich to the airport. Once Kloten airport was connected to both the national highway and railway networks (1980), the abundance of infrastructure was followed by offices and back offices, logistics firms and big box retailers. The international service proletariat encounters working class and even rural pockets. Thus, the fabric of everyday life in places such as Wallisellen, Opfikon, or Glattbrugg is characterized by a remarkably un-Swiss clash of programs, people, and typologies.

Redirecting conceptual energies

The political and institutional patchwork was ill equipped to address the mutation experienced and still underway in large parts of Glatttal city. In many ways this periurban landscape of neither-nor presents a blend that is typical of the contemporary urban condition—a condition that is often characterized as post-Fordist because it no longer follows the more predictable patterns of growth, consumption, and social organization that were typical of the mid-twentieth century. One can consider Post-Fordism as a form of deregulation and reorganization of the economic and social spheres. The unstable or unpredictable element of economic dynamics seems to have led to a redirection of conceptual energies. It highly affects how we experience and negotiate space, and therefore how architects are given new tasks to organize such space, now often consulting the real estate industry on questions of identity and urbanity.

A structural manifestation of Post-Fordism—aligning it with Postmodernism in architecture—presents a wariness of the plan and a tendency toward the image. Instead, it favors scenarios that are capable of dealing with the fragmented nature of urban development—the prevailing condition in Zürich Nord. The Oerlikon redevelopment scheme was still premised on a universalistic notion of urban planning that was determined in a top-down process. Subsequently—and in large part due to the real estate crisis and economic restructuring—strategies were

devised to function in more localized and targeted ways, placing stronger emphasis on the infusion of identity into a generic instability. Commodifying such identity means deploying images in space and manufacturing a product that is geared toward single-object urbanism, as the recent redevelopment strategies in Zürich West have demonstrated.

I want to tie this post-Fordist *logic* to another urban landscape that was itself beholden to the issue of identity: West Berlin. Like in Zurich in 2012, a Summer Academy held in Berlin in 1977 brought in students from abroad to tackle the city's problematic urban context. The students came from Cornell University and their professor was Oswald Mathias Ungers; they would conduct a series of design experiments together, returning the following summer to complete a new plan for action for West Berlin. The outcome of these Summer Academies later became known as the *Green Archipelago*.

A discussion of edges, sprawl, and investor dynamics would seem antithetical due to the nature of the contained and over-subsidized city. Nevertheless, the 1970s can be seen as a transitional period regarding the production and performance of architectural objects. At the time of Ungers' Summer Academies, West Berlin was witnessing a paradigm change that predates the recent impact of Post-Fordism and Globalization on cities and regions. It is no coincidence that the scheme was initially named *Cities within the City*, with the more metaphorical Archipelago serving only as subtitle for the eleven theses published in 1977. •1, ↗ Fig. 3, 4 First and foremost, a critique of the monolithic planning logic of late functionalism was intended, hence the emphasis on the multitude of Berlin's neighborhoods and their specific characteristics. **As a product of its time, the Green Archipelago envisioned a landscape of differences that took into account the social and economic realities of a deindustrialized city.** That Ungers hoped for a political impact is evident in his presentation of the work of the Summer Academy to the West Berlin Senate and in his tactical suggestion to host an international building exhibition. •2 Economically, West Berlin was a depleted city with no real economy and very little private building activity. In this regard, there is a stark difference to the booming region of Zurich North.

Evidently, the attempt to rethink the urban condition as a collection of islands within one large, contained territory was highly specific to the walled city. Why, then, has this somewhat forgotten scheme attracted such public attention in recent years? What might it have to say for the Zurich metropolitan area today? **The Green Archipelago was an attempt at authoring disjointed episodes—at giving them form in a relational system that, although fragmented, would be read as a composition, as an urban artifact.** Essential to the island metaphor was the idea that the isolation of distinctive elements would be capable of articulating specific urban qualities in condensed form. This potential was not merely attributed to the pre-1914 architectural legacy—a reductionism that would flourish after the reunification.

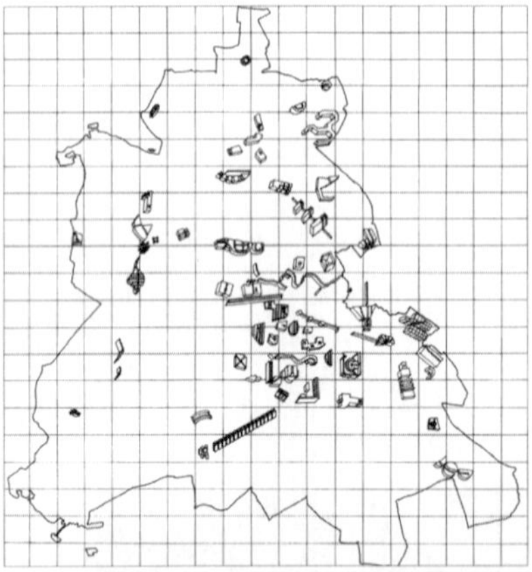

3 "Plan of selective urban islands" for West Berlin, from: *Die Stadt in der Stadt. Berlin das Grüne Stadtarchipel*, Cologne 1977

4 Peter Riemann: fragments within the Green Archipelago (1977)

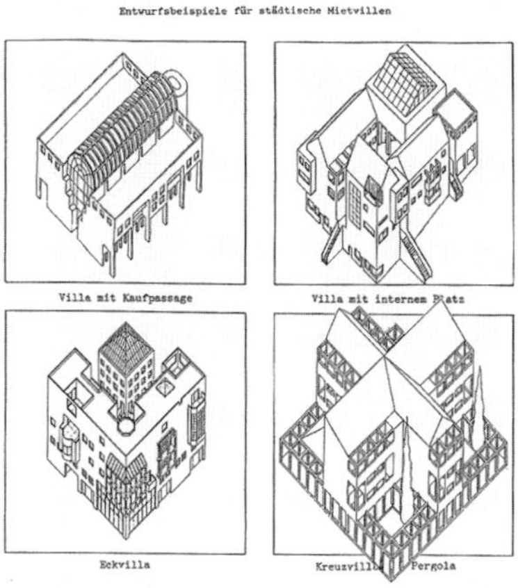

5 Prototypical housing studies from *The Urban Villa* (1977)

Berlin: a legacy of ideas and concepts

The curated urban landscape of the 1977 Archipelago drawings included the flotsam of the post-war welfare state. By representing the Märkisches Viertel—mass housing of which Ungers had been one of the designers—the architect acknowledged that his own architecture had become a recent chapter in Berlin's troubled history. Such a curatorial sensibility toward the city inverted the late modernist obsession with non-hierarchical systems and patterns—again, a discourse in which Ungers himself had participated.

Premised on the fragmentary, the Green Archipelago established a dialectics of infrastructure and architecture.

Culling from the on-site research of the Summer Academies, the shattered fabric of Berlin was mapped in order to generate a new whole. Isolated highways and decontextualized buildings were perceived as bearers of identity in the urban void. The many aborted or traumatized episodes of Berlin's history were seen as representing a rich legacy of ideas and concepts, exemplifying the theses of *Cities in the City*. Its authors voiced their criticism of the suppression of plurality for which they blamed both functionalist and new urbanist (*Stadtreparatur*) models. As *monolithic* concepts, Functionalism and *Stadtreparatur* were seen as stifling difference and, hence, considered to be antithetical to urbanity. Their normativity was seen as especially problematic in the hands of West Berlin's housing bureaucracy, where the welfare state was blamed for contributing to a passive mentality amongst the inhabitants. Therefore, both Cornell Summer Academies dismissed the premise of continuous growth, hoping to reposition the housing issue through new forms of agency and authorship.

More than the proposal for a post-industrial picturesque, the Green Archipelago also sought to stimulate local initiative. The proposal for home ownership and participatory planning models was based on the intermediate scale of the *Urban Villa*. ↗ Fig. 5 A concoction based on various historical precedents, this typological hybrid had been the focus of the first of the two Summer Academies. The *Urban Villa* then became a key ingredient of the Green Archipelago's dispersed urbanism. Synthesizing historical precedents—mainly taken from the *bürgerliche Stadt* of the nineteenth and early twentieth centuries—housing questions were approached from various urban traditions. Given the contemporary *desire* for *independence and free expression of personality*, the programmatic text co-authored by Ungers, Hans Kollhoff, and Arthur Ovaska after the 1977 Summer Academy identified a "typological vocabulary of formal richness" in historical precedents. •3 Socioeconomically, the Urban Villa was seen as a way to cater to an increasingly middle-class city with needs that could no longer be met by a housing policy based on standardization. Therefore, private initiative and home ownership were advocated as opportunities for a less universalistic, more community-oriented approach to housing. As prerequisites for a *pluralistic urban environment* in a shrinking city, the authors suggested increased citizen participation. Intended was a user-driven customization of the habitat, although the scaling back of state control of the building sector generally welcomed back market forces.

The issues surrounding the Urban Villa, in particular, the positive connotations of the free market, prepare the new reading of Berlin as a collection of *Cities within the City*. The Green Archipelago extolls

the multiplicity of *identity spaces* that would allow for the proliferation of a "differentiated urban structure" in terms of morphology, community, and usage. Again from a user-driven perspective, it also introduces the concept of urban farming to the walled city. The greening of Berlin encompasses multiple projections that reveal the surprising versatility of the metaphor and its authors. The frame of reference ranges from contemporary ecological awareness to historical precedents, such as the work of Peter Josef Lenné and Hans Scharoun in Berlin, also drawing from the genius loci, which had always been that of a verdant city.

Although fascinated by Prussian Romantic Classicism, Ungers offers an outlook far less prone to historicism than Rossi's contemporary *Città Analoga*. As a technique to edit the urban condition, the Green Archipelago was far more malleable than Rossi's division of the city into primary and secondary elements, which contrasted monuments and everyday fabric. Rossi was beholden to a view of the urban organism as an artifact where fixed points represented the presence of history, acting as the soul of an urban fabric that, beyond these sites of permanence and collective memory, was given over to permanent evolution. For Ungers, however, identity was not automatically assigned to the monumental edifice. Identity *could* be located in the monument, but his urban experience drew from the power of accidental and fragmentary encounters. This sensibility enabled Ungers to pay tribute to the havoc of the twentieth century and its double vectors of destruction—the random acts of demolition of World War II and post-war and contemporary planning, which more often than not had also resulted in a fragmentary and arbitrary liquidation of urban fabric. For this reading there is another frame of reference: the U.S. city. Ungers was confronted with the United States in a period of severe crisis. He began to teach at Cornell University at a time when U.S. downtowns were going up in flames following the assassination of Martin Luther King Jr. in April 1968. The acute urban crisis occurred after an already extended implosion based on destructive urban renewal policies and the economic consequences of white flight to suburbia.

Like the failing fabric in many U.S. inner cities, the Urban Villa and the Green Archipelago revolved around a dialectic of growth and decay that was largely premised on market forces. Given Ungers' later formalism that was buttressed by his erudite defense of *architecture as architecture*, such a socioeconomic penchant appears unusual. Immersed in the academia of 1970s North America, he was immune to both the formal bricolage of Colin Rowe's *Collage City* and the fetishization of pop culture in *Learning from Las Vegas* by Robert Venturi, Denise Scott Brown, and Steven Izenour.

To fully clarify the U.S. undercurrent in Ungers' answer to urban failure requires a return to the perceptual lessons of Kevin Lynch in the late 1950s. Analyzing the distressed downtowns of U.S. cities, *The Image of the City* had clearly pointed out the deficiencies of functionalist urbanism. In research that mined the potentials of a new spatio-visual organization, Lynch called for qualities such as "environmental imageability" and a "coincidence of association and imageability." [4] Ironically, Ungers had also been exposed to the U.S. inner city prior to his arrival in the U.S. The key figure in bringing Lynch's ideas to Germany was Thomas Sieverts, the same man who, several decades later, coined the term *Zwischenstadt* and ran the IBA Emscher Park. In the mid-1960s Sieverts was still a teaching assistant at TU Berlin where he introduced Lynch's ideas of imageability and visual mapping into planning studios that were co-hosted together with Ungers' own chair, the site of legendary studio experiments and publications from 1963 on. As a covert influence, Lynch appears in a photographic study of contemporary Berlin that was conducted by Ungers' chair, prior to his departure for Cornell, and published in 1969. •5

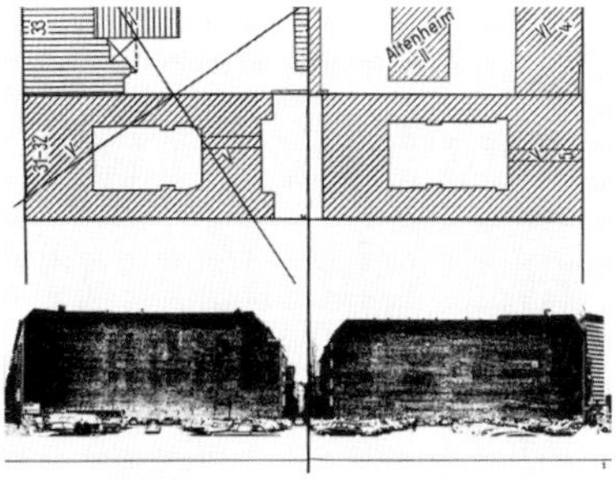

6 Party walls and cadastral information from the study by Prof. Unger's chair at Technische Universität Berlin, *Berliner Brandwände*, Berlin 1969

7 Concrete cooling towers, Bernd und Hilla Becher

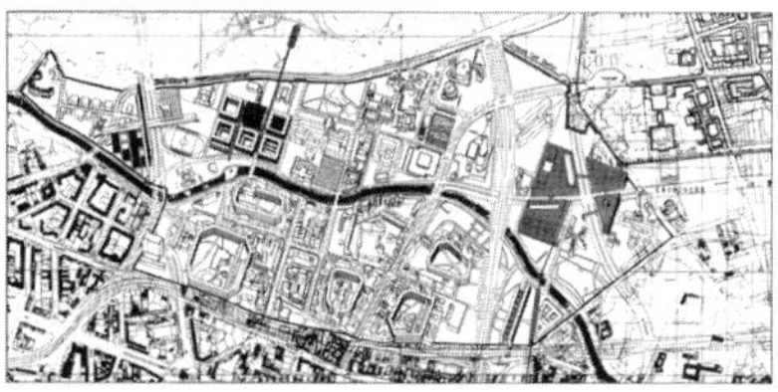

8 O. M. Ungers with Rem Koolhaas: Berlin Tiergarten idea competion (1973)

Planning in the petri dish

Berlin Party Walls is surely one of the most startling documents in Ungers' evolution. A combined photographic and cartographic survey of the matrix of the nineteenth-century tenement city, it presents an urban taxonomy premised on the random acts of destruction of the war, which, in West Berlin of the 1960s, could still be experienced in the form of countless exposed blank surfaces. ↗ Fig. 6 Berlin Party Walls is dominated by grainy images taken by photographer Arthur Laskus of accidental, windowless elevations. The publication prominently features these jarring X-rays of the structural logic behind often violent processes of urbanization. Aligned with cadastral plans, the photographic spreads reveal the economic reality underpinning the nineteenth-century Mietskaserne tenements. The party wall, a formerly hidden layer of information peeled open by bombing, almost offers premonition of the work of Gordon Matta Clark. One can also relate the Berlin survey to the context of contemporary work, such as Ed Ruscha's *Every Building on the Sunset Strip* or Dan Graham's *Homes for America*, two potent narratives dealing with consumption and urbanization in mid-1960s America.

Ungers was an avid art collector, and, closer to home, there are obvious ties to Bernd and Hilla Becher, whose works he had in his collection. Their sensibility for the vernacular of gas tanks, furnaces, and water towers is indeed the counterpart to the *objets trouvés* of Berlin's depressed real estate. ↗ Fig. 7 Akin to the Bechers' photographic inventory of the everyday, the force of repetition in Berlin Party Walls transforms the nineteenth- and early twentieth-century tenements into a typological prop. Isolated in the thinned and barren urban landscape, speculative architecture is suddenly endowed with an abstract, almost sculptural aura. Prepared by his teaching assistants at TU, Berlin Party Walls still lacked a design agenda and made no attempts at a socioeconomic assessment of the urban condition. Nevertheless, the survey is an early and pivotal step toward a reading of the city as no longer predicated on quantitative growth, but increasingly defined by the distribution of symbols and markers.

Anticipating the Green Archipelago, Berlin Party Walls exposed shrinkage as a reality. Although it is still under-theorized, the emphasis on the presence of everyday iconic elements in a void cityscape can be seen as indebted to Lynch's perceptual involvement with the U.S. inner city. •6 Affirming, mapping, and staging the failure of the post-war city would become increasingly crucial for Ungers during the ten-year hiatus of his building practice while teaching in the U.S. From a distance, he began to process West Berlin as a collection of lost objects: a constellation of fragments

to be curated. A crucial step toward this formalization of non-coherence was the Tiergarten competition (1973) where Ungers collaborated with his Cornell graduate student Rem Koolhaas. ↗ Fig. 8 Similar to the Green Archipelago, the scheme assigns the function of conveying identity to strong markers in a park-like setting littered with historical and contemporary fragments. Situated in the vicinity of the Wall, the design curates these episodes along with their problematic context characterized by the twofold dystopia of war and post-war urban renewal. •7

As a survey of Berlin, the Green Archipelago takes disjuncture much further. It reveals competing episodes of modernity that range from working-class tenements, factories, and infrastructural fragments to the fortresses of the post-war welfare state, such as the Märkisches Viertel—the controversy over which caused Ungers to shy away from mass housing and contributed to his deep frustration with all public building commissions after 1968. The period leading up to the Summer Academies in Berlin also coincides with a period known as the *Red Decade* in West Germany. Beginning with the 1967 student protests in Berlin, culminating in the *Hot Autumn* of 1977 with the peak of terrorist activity by the Red Army Fraction, these ten traumatic years also encompass the research leading from Berlin Party Walls to the Green Archipelago. Was architecture production affected by this conflict, and how can Ungers' distant gaze at the condition of Germany be interpreted here?

On the one hand, the Red Decade was marked by a profound attack on the consensus of the Federal Republic, in particular, on the patriarchal traditions of the German welfare state. On the other hand, as the relationship between the two superpowers began to evolve, it affected the identity of West Berlin as key site of the Cold War. In the 1972 peace accords, the two German states acknowledged their mutual right to exist and initiate diplomatic relations. Although the Wall would continue to exist for nearly twenty years the contained urban territory lost its definition as frontier and showcase of the West. This geopolitical shift marks the beginning of a gradual de-politicization of space. Previously cast into the spotlight on either side of the Wall, all planning endeavors in the divided city had been magnified as though in a petri dish. From 1972 on, the late-modern super-project is no longer a necessary narrative to offset the *soziale Marktwirtschaft* of the Federal Republic from Socialism. Ungers himself had gravitated toward an enlightened Fordist technocracy in the mid-1960s when his curatorial approach toward the *broken* fabric of the city would have been anathema to his building practice. As the texts emerging from the Cornell Summer Academies demonstrate, their discourse on history, identity, and urban space is influenced by a political and economic dynamic. In the unique case of Berlin, political détente opens up architecture for new narratives, indirectly serving as a catalyst for the demise of hyper-functionalism. Coagulating dispersed urban fragments and authoring a new image for urban space is indicative of a re-appropriation of history.

By the time of the 1977 Summer Academy, Ungers was well aware that reclaiming and preserving the fabric of the nineteenth century are ways to gain reentry into the building market.

Soon after the European Year of Preservation (1975) and in the wake of preservation legislation, but also based on federal subsidization of inner-city reinvestment, West Berlin subscribed to the formula of *Behutsame Stadterneuerung*, literally: cautious urban renewal. In order to overcome the cultural crisis, public and subsidized housing would soon be tied to the same identity politics as urban governance. Both the Green Archipelago and Urban Villa texts register the increased importance of more subjective, soft factors for a differentiated consumer society. The reoccupation of urban space and its inhabitation by heterogeneous scenes was the indirect legacy of 1968. Here, the *identity spaces* that informed the metaphor of Cities within the City appear to be more in tune with the discourse of community of the U.S. neighborhood than with the traditional interventionism of the German welfare state. •8

Staging difference-promoting visions

Before he was consumed by his own rigorous, hermetic discourse, Ungers seized the opportunity to define a new rapport between the self, the habitat, and urban space. In the transitional period of the 1970s, West Berlin proved to be a unique environment to reposition architecture. **As a metaphor, the Green Archipelago has experienced a surprising renaissance in the past decade, re-appropriated and instrumentalized, although in a very productive way.** In all the excitement over these ideas from the 1970s, the overall context in which Ungers' urban imaginary evolved has been obscured, if not distorted. Not only did the Archipelago entail a shift away from industrialized mass housing *per se*; consciously, perhaps subconsciously, Ungers anticipated a form of spectatorship that would become essential for the repositioning of the architect as *auteur* in the postmodern city.

Pier Vittorio Aureli has appropriated the Archipelago to mount his "metacritique of urbanization." •9 In a series of writings, he casts the metaphor of Cities in the City as a defense shield against a rampant process of generic, global urbanization. For Aureli, the finiteness of the individual fragment with robust boundaries becomes a tactic to resist contamination by Post-Fordism's pervasive forces. Clearly, Ungers also has a particular sympathy with the formal rigor of *inertia*: Aureli contrasts *absolute architecture* with parametrized design aesthetics that he sees as the outcome of a cultural production impoverished by relativization. Responding to the same situation that is criticized by Aureli, Kees Christiaanse has revisited the Archipelago metaphor as a strategy for a more flexible planning practice, to instigate and leverage local identity with *atmospheric enclaves* whose experiential quality has become a commodity in itself. Globalization is typically criticized for having obliterated the specific qualities of places. Meeting the needs of real estate developers increasingly means establishing an address for volatile programs. Under the premises of *the city as loft*, Christiaanse deploys the Archipelago as a useful tool to harness multiple unknown factors in contemporary planning processes. •10 Multiplicity becomes an asset because it no longer implies negotiating an overall morphology. In the hands of the tactician of countless urban plans, the Archipelago accommodates the global capital of what David Harvey calls *flexible accumulation*.

Ungers and his collaborators did not fully address the issue of implementation. Yet as a curatorial strategy, the Archipelago will always be tied to the question of the power governing a given territory. In today's competing metropolitan regions, the expression and negotiation of power is distinctly different as compared with the period of the Summer Academies in Berlin. The New York sociologist Sharon Zukin has argued that power is already exerted when a certain group is able to articulate and promote a vision for urban space. •11 According to Zukin, control over space resides increasingly in the ability to provide an image that convincingly conveys a form of identity with interests particularly vested in the construction of an "ambiance of authenticity." •12 Once an image is successfully established, a space becomes accessible for private capital. Although Zukin's viewpoint of radical commodification strongly reflects the dynamics of real estate and gentrification in the United States, the transformation of Zürich Nord is exposed to a similar force field. Programs are dictated by the increasingly global standards of a service industry and the professionals in its wake.

A periurban landscape of neither-nor, shaped by networks of high mobility, global capital, and sparse remnants of traditional industry and craftsmanship, blends different temporalities between the edges of Oerlikon, Kloten airport, and Wallisellen. Mining the catalysts of identity and urbanity, architects are the service professionals of localization, driven by the private sector to add ever more features to the urban landscape. In turn, this inflation of difference reinforces fragmentation, doing little to articulate an overall identity. Clearly, this is a problem of political scale and governance, compounded by the intricate stop-and-go of Swiss direct democracy. There is still little evidence about who might constitute the public of a future Glatttal city and even about whom planning is meant to address there. A clear answer may be antithetical to the elusive nature of Post-Fordism. But the grey area between the generic and the specific is where spatial tactics are called for.

Endnotes

•1 Co-authored with his assistants and first released by Ungers' own "Studioverlag für Architektur": Oswald Mathias Ungers, Rem Koolhaas, Peter Riemann, Hans Kollhoff, Arthur Ovaska, *Die Stadt in der Stadt. Berlin, das grüne Stadtarchipel. Ein stadträumliches Planungskonzept für die zukünftige Entwicklung Berlins*, Cologne 1977, subsequently as: *Cities within the City: Proposals by the Summer Academy for Berlin*, *Lotus*, no. 19, 1978. Co-hosted by the West Berlin International Centre for Design, the Cornell Summer Academies enabled on-site research for Ungers and his group of teaching assistants and students. "The Urban Villa" was followed by "The Urban Garden" in 1978; a third academy, dealing with the topic of public art and the city, did not take place.

•2 Not only was such a project underway in Berlin by 1979, when the *Internationale Bauausstellung* was approved, Ungers was also appointed as one of its commissioners. However, he soon resigned from this position. The explanations for this move range from the rivalry with fellow commissioner Josef Paul Kleihues to the desire to resume his practice within the IBA.

•3 Oswald Mathias Ungers, Hans Kollhoff, and Arthur Ovaska, *The Urban Villa: A Multi-family Dwelling Type*, Cologne 1977. The publication of the results in Ungers' own press was followed in 1978 by Lotus where, alongside the Archipelago mappings and various case studies, the eleven theses were featured: Oswald Mathias Ungers, Rem Koolhaas, Peter Riemann, Hans Kollhoff, and Arthur Ovaska, *Cities within the City: Proposals by the Summer Academy for Berlin*, *Lotus*, no. 19, 1978

•4 Kevin Lynch, *The Image of the City*, Cambridge 1960, pp. 13, 101

•5 *Berliner Brandwände, Veröffentlichungen zur Architektur* no. 27, TU Berlin (ed.), Lehrstuhl für Entwerfen VI, Berlin 1969. His discovery of the *Veröffentlichungen zur Architektur*, released by Ungers' chair at TU Berlin until 1970, was a reason for Rem Koolhaas to study with Ungers at Cornell.

•6 The "as found" perspective of Berlin Party Walls was somewhat indebted to Team Ten, with whom Ungers had maintained an informal but ongoing relationship—especially with Alison and Peter Smithson whom he would invite to Berlin and later to Cornell University.

•7 On the Berlin Tiergarten Scheme, see: André Bideau, *Elusive Ungers*, AA Files 64/2012

•8 For a broader discussion of the question of identity and urban space in Germany during this period: André Bideau, *Architektur und symbolisches Kapital. Bilderzählungen und Identitätsproduktion bei O. M. Ungers*, Basel 2011

•9 Pier Vittorio Aureli, *The Project of Autonomy. Politics and Architecture within and against Capitalism*, New York 2008

•10 Kees Christiaanse, *Ein Grüner Archipel – Ein Berliner Stadtkonzept revisited*, Disp, 156/2004; Kees Christiaanse et al., *The City as Loft*, KCAP/ASTOC exhibition catalogue, NAI, Rotterdam 2003

•11 Sharon Zukin, *The Cultures of Cities*, Cambridge 1995, p. 297

•12 Sharon Zukin, *Landscapes of Power—from Detroit to Disney World*, Berkeley 1991, p. 51

Text based on lecture delivered on July 30, 2012
at the International Summer Academy Zurich

Schlieren

Ulrich Görlich & Meret Wandeler

2005

2007

2009

2011 (Schlieren, Bachstrasse, Geissweid site, looking north-west)

The photographs are from the research project “Long-Term Photographic Observation of Schlieren,” directed by Ulrich Görlich and Meret Wandeler at the Institute for Contemporary Art Research at Zurich University of the Arts (*www.beobachtung-schlieren.ch*). The series of images shows the step-by-step development of well-served areas along the railway line and close to the center as an example of the process of inward-growing densification in Schlieren. This is an important goal of the urban development concept of Metron Raumentwicklung AG and forms the starting point for the photographic documentation.

Text based on lecture delivered on July 31, 2012
at the International Summer Academy Zurich

In a postmodern, fragmented society, what kind of ideology should be the software for rebuilding our new cities?

Architects Group Krokodil

It is paradoxical: it is precisely the indestructible rural souls of the Swiss that are destroying the country. Even under great pressure we don't wish to become urbanites. We don't want to move closer together.

Marcel Meili

It's more likely caused by the continued effect of the modernist ideology, which to this day makes it impossible for many to believe in the city. The greenery, the distance, the view: these are the qualities of the modernist city that we universally don't want to do without.

Emanuel Christ & Christoph Gantenbein

We will understand, if not show, the possibilities of multiple readings, of maps that do not align immediately.

Arno Brandlhuber, Christopher Roth & Sam Chermayeff

When it's necessary to create something new, to conceive an invention of the future, then paradoxically only one thing is available to the architect: the past.

Emanuel Christ & Christoph Gantenbein

Measuring the surface of the earth is the basis of all building activities. Land as a resource is partitioned, possessed, traded, or intentionally excluded from market mechanisms.

Anne-Julchen Bernhardt & Jörg Leeser

You can't plan without getting your hands dirty.

Anne-Julchen Bernhardt & Jörg Leeser

Studio A
Lecturers Arno Brandlhuber, Christopher Roth, Sam Chermayeff
Students Sarah Föry, Rahel Horisberger, Magdalena Krapfenbauer, Fabian Lackinger, Caspar Lundsgaard-Hansen, Hannah Müller, Alexandra Razina, Christopher Rieke, Maarten van Kesteren, Caroline Vogel, Nikolas von Schwabe

When the three of us first met, one was against planning, one was for planning, and the third was in between. We all agreed on connecting Zurich with C. G. Jung and the Austrian Nobel Laureate Wolfgang Pauli and their search to reunite the psyche and physics. Their thinking portended a theory of everything based on complementarity, as in Heisenberg's famous principle: at the atomic level there is always a correlation between two physical entities. If one measures a thing very closely, the complementary disappears, a law of nature. The sharper you illuminate an object, the deeper the shadows fall.

On the first day of our course we went to the restaurant *Krokodil* to get an impression of our host's founding legend. The Spanish place was closed for holidays and we made a group photo in front of a huge paella image there. On the second day we walked from the Pauli ETH institute on the hill down to the Jung institute by the lake. We mostly talked about the possible complementary opposites of planning. It was not de-construction; it was not the void, or even observation. More likely it had to do with games, stages, performance, celebration, or the possibility of doing nothing, politely. (We still miss these discussions very much.)

The great philosopher of our time, Jamie Oliver, said he would never have expected to mix fish and meat in one dish. Here we were back to paella. We cooked some different versions in black and red, an Indian one, and finally one that we shared with the whole Summer Academy. Redefining the space with a camera, a beamer, a Skype connection (to Brandlhuber and Carson Chan cooking in Berlin), and the idea of celebration and performance. Jung and Pauli made *quaternios*—plans for synthesizing the *conjunctio*, as they called it. Each was a cross with, for example, the complementarities of space and time on the vertical axis and causality and synchronicity on the horizontal. Or, we considered The Prime Tower and the Bollingen Tower (C. G. Jung) as another. Looking at *quaternio*, in the second week everybody worked on her or his own, which became personal statements that attempted to define multiple truths in one point of view. We made one-shot films—starting with ten-minutes, then five minutes, three and finally one and a half. It was a presentation of a hypothesis based on the idea of complementarity and the "4."

Chess Match

C. G. Jung and his wife

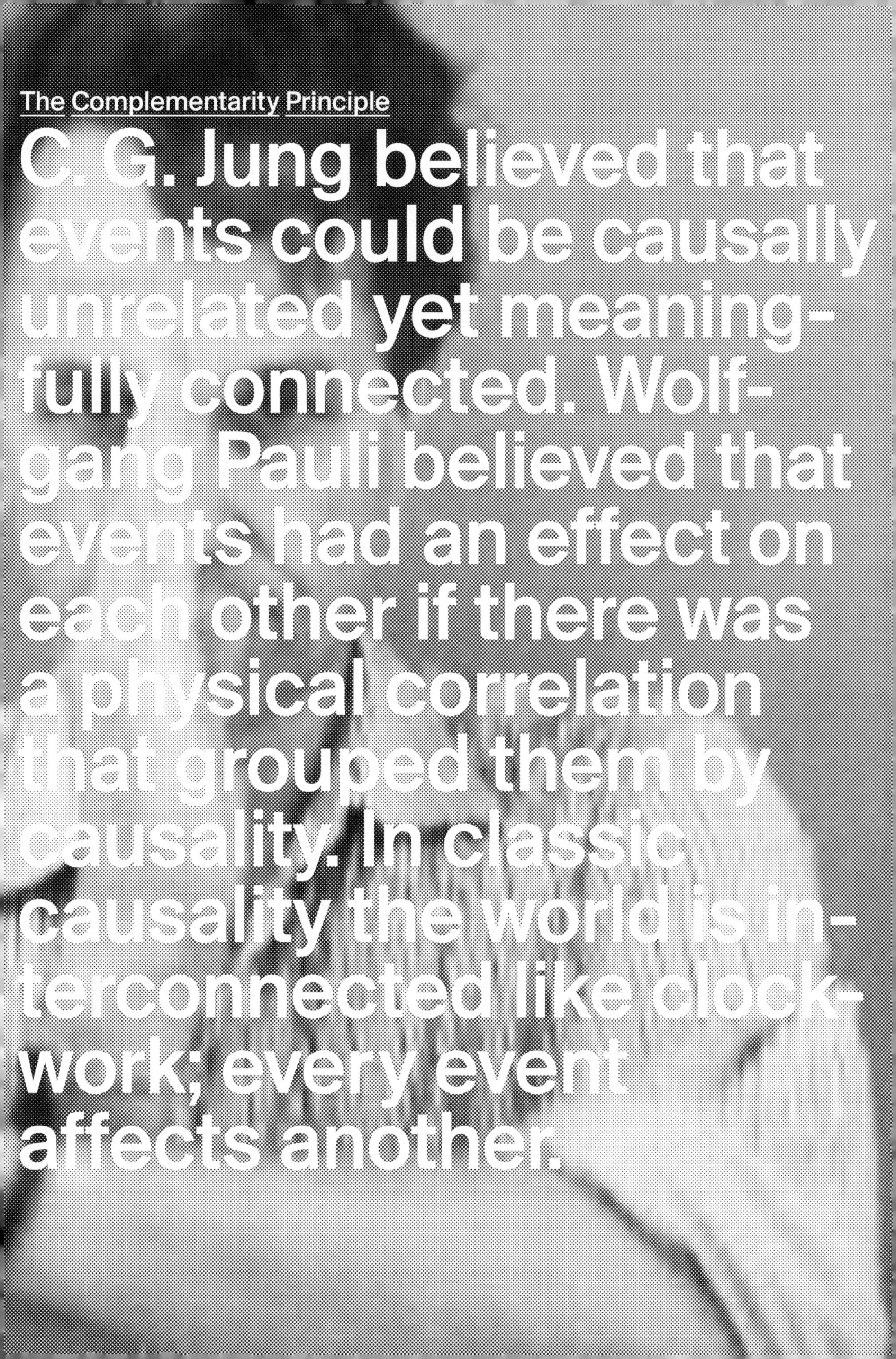

The Complementarity Principle

C. G. Jung believed that events could be causally unrelated yet meaning-fully connected. Wolf-gang Pauli believed that events had an effect on each other if there was a physical correlation that grouped them by causality. In classic causality the world is in-terconnected like clock-work; every event affects another.

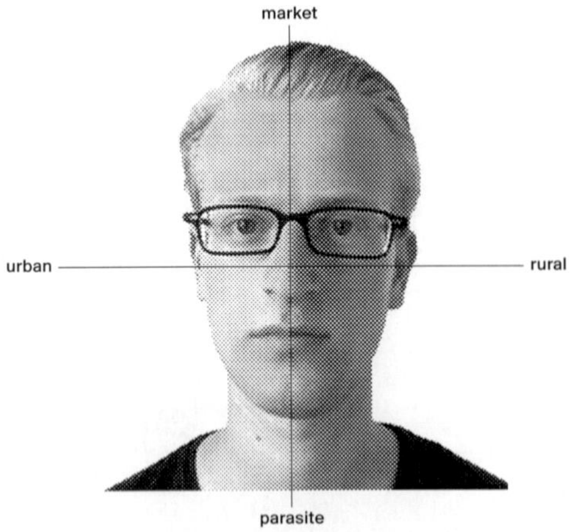

Christopher Rieke (CR)

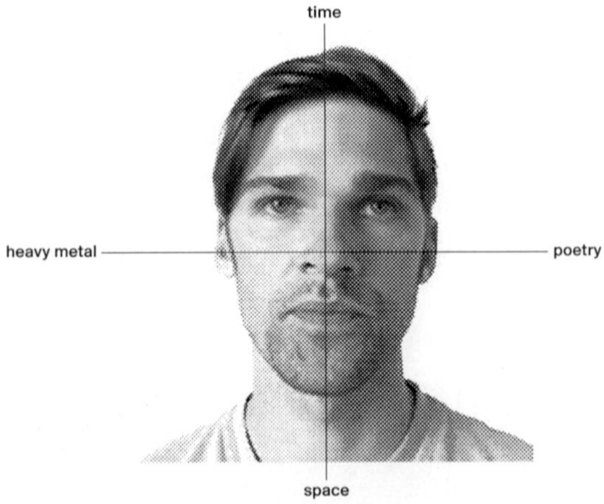

Fabian Lackinger (FL)

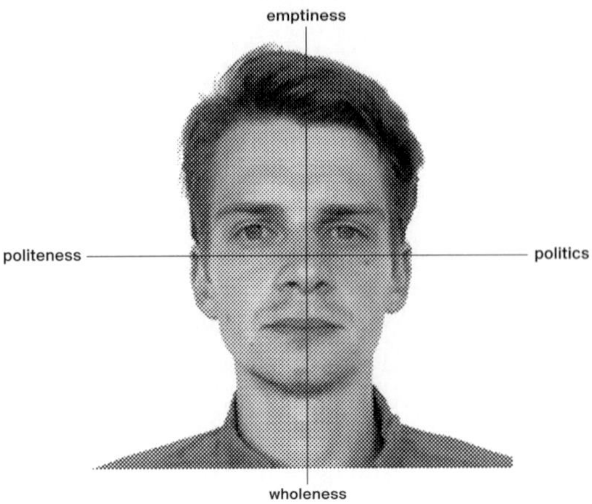

Nikolas von Schwabe (NvS)

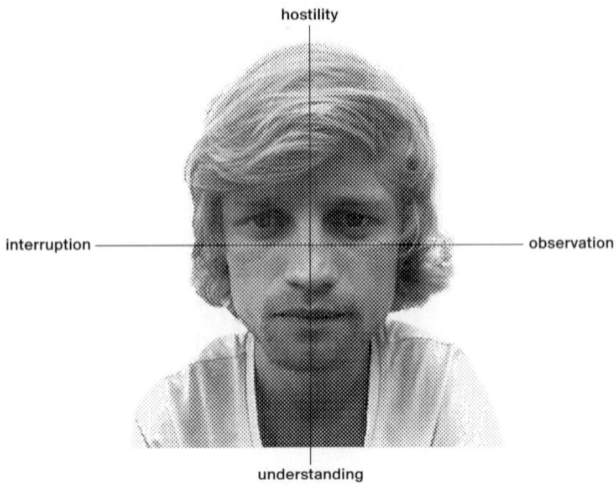

Maarten van Kesteren (MvK)

The traditional European city can be described as a city of consumption, which relates to one constitutional property of the urban culture: The market idea as the ordered, controlled, urban exchange platform within certain fixed rules of giving and taking goods, information, knowledge, political responsibility, and also space in a very immediate way.

This depicted organizational process needs and has always created a certain kind of planning attitude of the urban, which affects and also depends on its complementary—the rural—and vice versa. So intervention and stimulation, such as space exchange, never includes just one of the two sides.
… Putting content parts into new context parts in order to generate new meaning layers that would affect their surroundings. So this parasitic stimulation would then create new situations instead of creating new forms. • CR

Heavy metal represents a strong attitude without being able to offer you a strong support, which leaves all options open. In this sense a chorus out of this genre goes literally: "Resistance is useless. Uselessness is art. Art is resisting. Resistance is useless."

There must be space for different ritual spaces and their celebration—not only in the urban discourse but also in its execution. • FL

My hypothesis is that politeness is a very important ingredient of a society. Politeness, simply understood as the practical application of good manners, is complementary to politics. This means the more you focus on politics, the further you are from politeness and vice-versa.

… This strictly executed top-down political decision is that they left behind the billboard frames without content as an artifact … the emptiness created in this way opens up the possibility to self-project one's own ideas onto this polite emptiness … as long as one is able to recognize the absence of the billboards, one is able to redefine a whole new subjective Wholeness as complementary to emptiness. • NvS

Not being able to understanding something creates hostility. This also works the other way around, because hostility closes the mind to really understanding something.

The act of observing something changes the picture of reality and reality itself. These thoughts can also be projected onto planning in which observing and interruption are main parameters. Planning can evoke hostility and understanding. Connecting the dots previously drawn, one can then conclude that there is no indifference within planning. • MvK

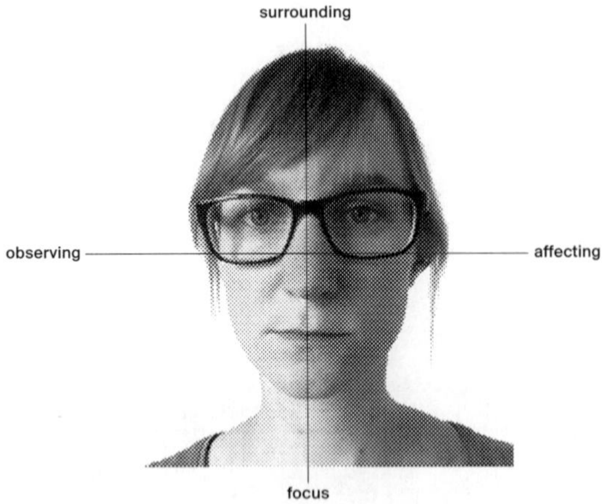

Sarah Föry (SF)

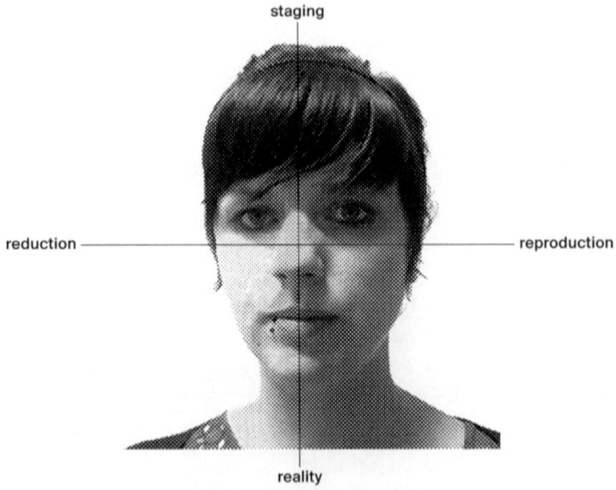

Hannah Müller (HM)

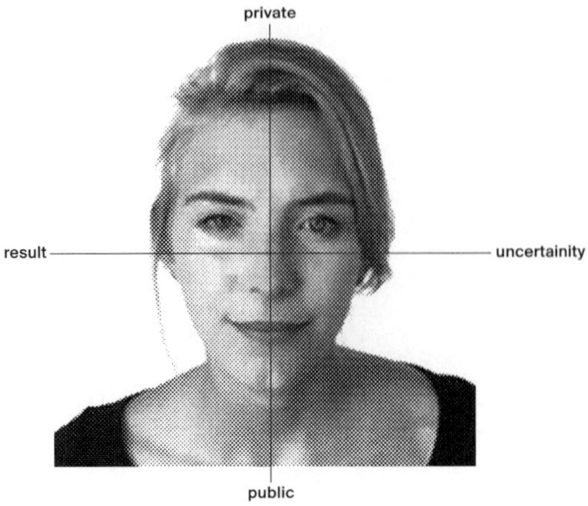

Magdalena Krapfenbauer (MK)

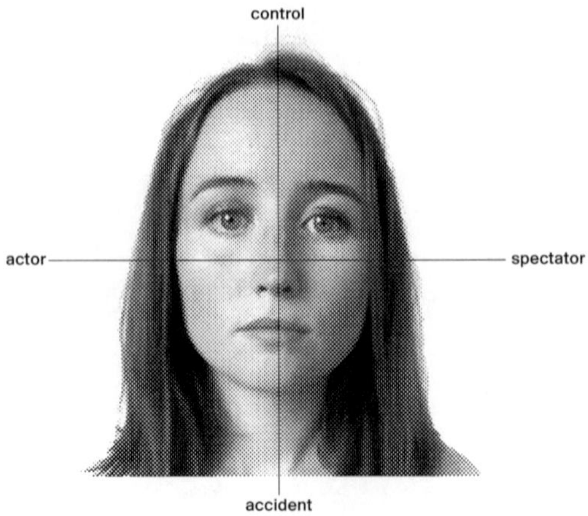

Alexandra Razina (AR)

A heterotopia is always part of reality but with its own reality inside. And they are never static. They depend on each other.

The surroundings observe these other places and become affected by them. In this way the focus acts like a virus that has an impact on its surroundings. The surroundings of the boat are also an island. It's a heterotopia for the fish. You just have to change your point of view! • SF

The complementarities reduction and reproduction, stage and reality have a strong connection to each other.

Therefore, I assume that media stages reality. Today, due to globalization, the world is growing closer together. We have easy access to information about events taking place on the other side of the world, without actually being there or taking part. But there is always somebody directing which information is being transmitted from the sender to receiver and how it is transmitted, using instruments such as reducing or reproducing. Reality becomes a product of media—or the stage becomes reality after a while. Reality is being formed and shaped by what is shown through media, and Santa Claus becomes more real than the Tiananmen massacre. • HM

Given the courageous goal of planning and organizing everything correctly, the risk of a static situation based on society's behavior and facilitation through technological developments is often practically guaranteed. In this context, a quick excurse to a new social trend, called "Quantify Self Movement" can be quite revealing.

How is it possible that the creation of technological tools and public response can have such an impact on the self-awareness of followers who want more control over their lives? The comfortable situation of stability removes the fear of uncertainty, but also personal freedom and the option of getting to results by trying and finding other possibilities. • MK

So what is the role of a person in the process of planning? Generally, people are conservative and don't like changes. They are spectators, because only a spectator makes his own reality and has control over it.

In that unplanned, individual reality there is no understanding of an accident. Only in the moment a planning process appears the accident has sense, but all people become actors. And even a real town is just a decoration. • AR

Studio E

Lecturers Anne-Julchen Bernhardt, Jörg Leeser
Students Pau Bajet, Földvàry Balàzs, Isabel Glogar, Eva Roll, Andrew Segovia, Anastasia Vaynberg, Lilly Zheng

Plat studio focused on land partition as a mechanism of urban growth. The scale of the studio's activities ranged from new dormer windows to new city centers. Analyzing the early twentieth-century movement of Freiland, we found hints for the future development of Glatttal and the airfield in particular. Plat studio is generative research of Glatttal's transformation from a semi-intentional assortment of differently sized and shaped lots to something yet to be discovered. Property lines become the crucial design tool when clod turns into plot. Plat studio has looked at the inherent conditions of settlement from every appropriate angle. We tried to anticipate the emergence of new agglomerative typologies, embarking on an endeavor to marry suburban contextualism with the apparent *tabula rasa* of the airfield. At stake is no less than a universal formula for the still underexplored territories of agglomeration.

"We now ought to deal with the existing boundaries in order to save what can still be saved. In other words: all the beautiful and good things that emerge from studies of old towns, all the wonderful designs for new, unheard-of creations at present lack the main thing, the ground and the land on which they can be created and where they can later freely develop." (Hans Bernoulli, *Die Stadt und ihr Boden*, Zurich, 1946, pp. 7–8)

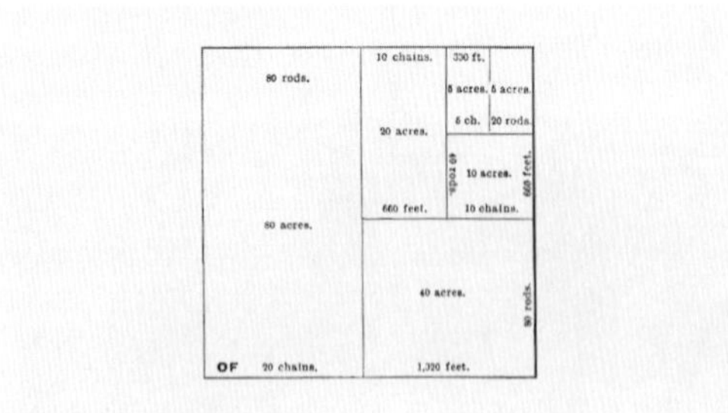

Thomas Jefferson, Territorial Partition of the USA, Land Ordinance of 1785

Oklahoma Land Rush, 1889

Plat Studio

Developing strategies for a Glatttal Plat plan, but also aimed to generate new urban typologies derived from conditions of local sprawl.

Core Area Airfield: Dübendorf, Wangen-Brüttisellen, and Volketswil

Plot plan airfield

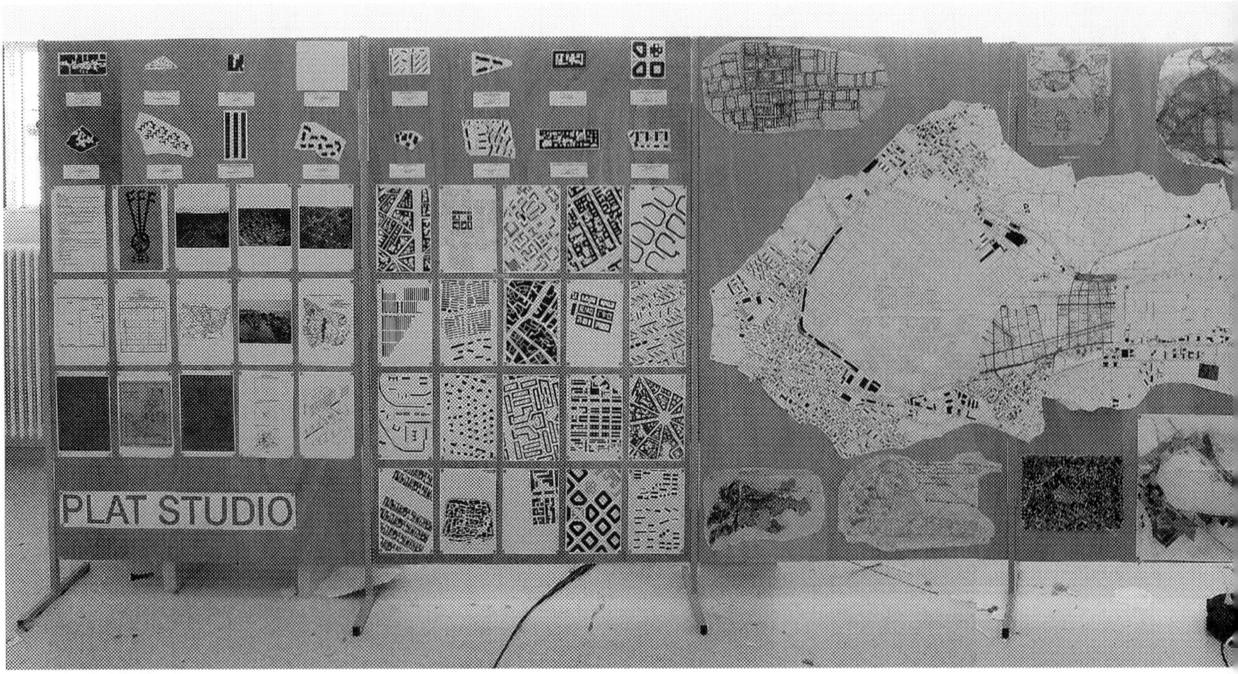

Presentation wall Plat Studio

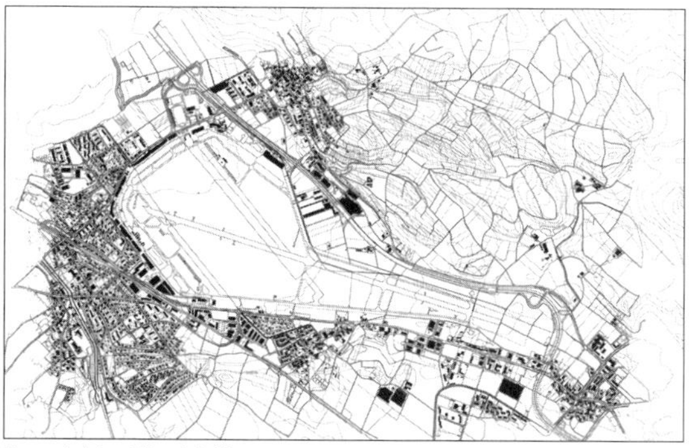
Present state of the airfield

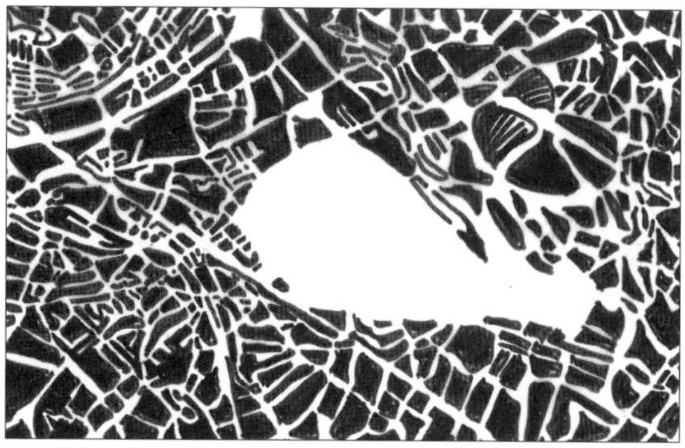
Plot structure of the surroundings

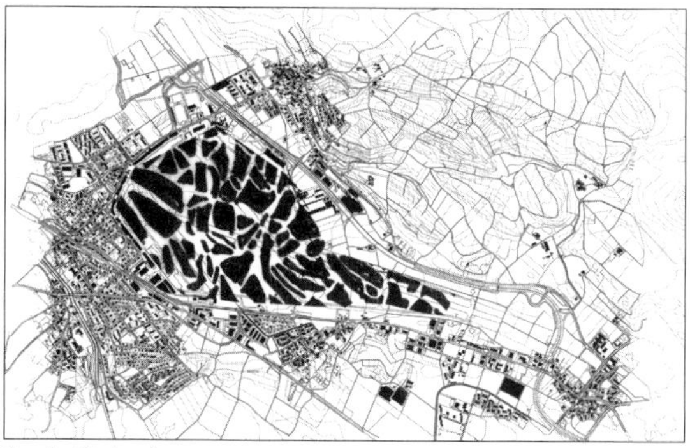
Result of the input

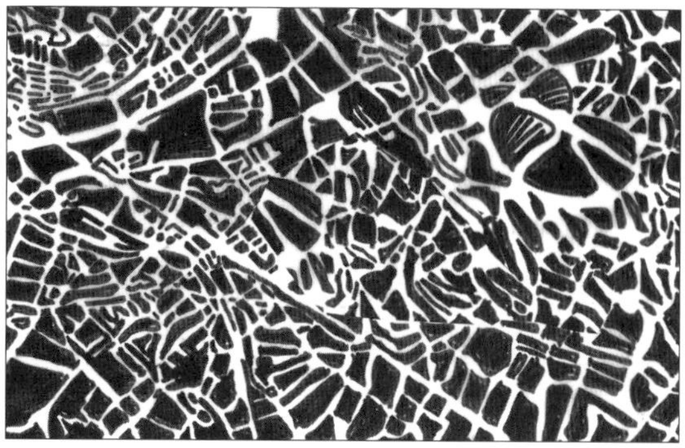
Input of the structure to the airfield

Urban density and attractive forms of public transportation networks are interdependent. What is the urban potential of such networks?

Architects Group Krokodil

Today we need to reassess our ambitions of mobility and admit that until now, mobility has not been successfully urbanized—congestion is the rule for any large city.

Alfredo Brillembourg & Hubert Klumpner

... Like many developing cities, it is also characterized by pollution, overpopulation, and paralysis—"Glatt is a developing city."

Kunlé Adeyemi

Glatttal is constructed around a mono-functional transport infrastructure, whose lack of human scale and design quality form well-documented barriers between districts.

Alfredo Brillembourg & Hubert Klumpner

The commuter railway alone does not establish a city, but, at most, a way of life. Consequently, the question arises as to who should give the territory its form.

Marcel Meili

Nineteenth century = horizontal, twentieth century = vertical, twenty-first century = diagonal.

Alfredo Brillembourg & Hubert Klumpner

A return to 100-percent-pedestrian cities.

David Trottin

Studio D
Lecturers Alfredo Brillembourg, Hubert Klumpner
Assistant Lea Ruefenacht
Students Jarolím Antal, Itamar Bergfreund, Rogerio Cruz Oliveira, Lara Ferreira, Lorenzo Figna, Frieder Kaiser, Julia Kick, Bence Komlosi, Olavi Kukk, Tien Ling, Pegah Noori Khah, Lucia Pennati, Paula Prkačin, Farrah Sabouni, Valeria Zamora Marco

Urban-Think Tank's approach for the Summer Academy Studio 2012 was to expand the understanding of movement and connectivity by inventing multi-functional objects that could rearticulate and redefine the relationship within a dense urban environment. It brought multi-scalar mobility concepts into existence that could transform basic movement into a dynamic and synchronized chain of activities. Through the creation of multi-functional transition spaces for interaction and exchange, these networked hubs would serve as access and connection points for increased mobility and social engagement.

To understand mobility, one must understand human behavior and movement as a dynamic and perpetually changing process. Urban life depends on places that allow people to meet, exchange, and coexist. As this has been dramatically challenged by the dominant culture of car ownership and rapid urbanization during the twentieth century, Urban-Think Tank's approach aimed at developing concepts that could reinvigorate urban space and project new scenarios for the future. Participants analyzed, speculated, probed, and constructed a jointly developed overlapping project that dealt with a set of evolving mobility concepts, the product being a large-scale model—a *feasible utopia* in the words of Yona Friedman. The 1:100 model of 6x6 diameters formed the construction site, while simultaneously representing the conflicts and negotiations between projects.

By introducing and testing a diverse and dense urban fabric into the Glatttal area, the aim was to formulate a new urban vision for Glatttal: A vision that would exceed the promises of modernism by including the reality of congestion, while also helping to liberate design from the premise of the object. The aim was not to subjugate Glatttal to a prescribed package of errors derived from the conventional city planners' repertoire, but rather, to liberate design by redefining the role of architects and urbanists as curators of possibilities that are capable of critically examining conventional modes of planning.

The urban spaces were liberated from the conventional ground plan view of a city by engaging all possibilities of three-dimensional modes of mobility. Flexible territories were introduced, enabling the new city to support a spectrum of innovative programs and typologies accessible for self-determination and adaptation. New possibilities would emerge and permeate the dense fabric, allowing for the productive utilization of all spaces in new capacities. Within an asymmetrical urbanization process, this can be regarded as a key component for a more adaptive approach to urban planning.

Glatttal is constructed around a mono-functional transport infrastructure whose lack of human scale and design quality forms well-documented barriers between districts.

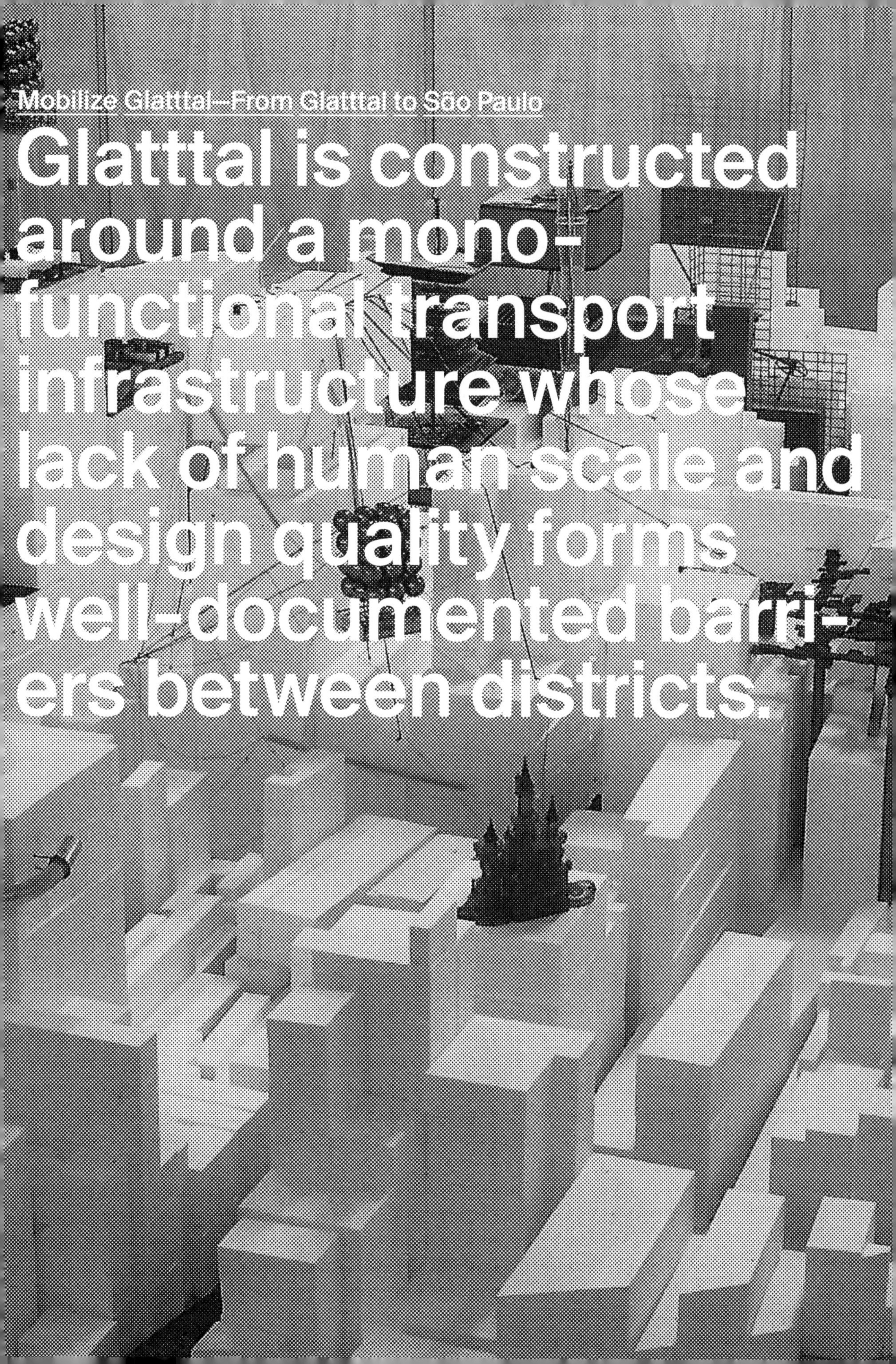

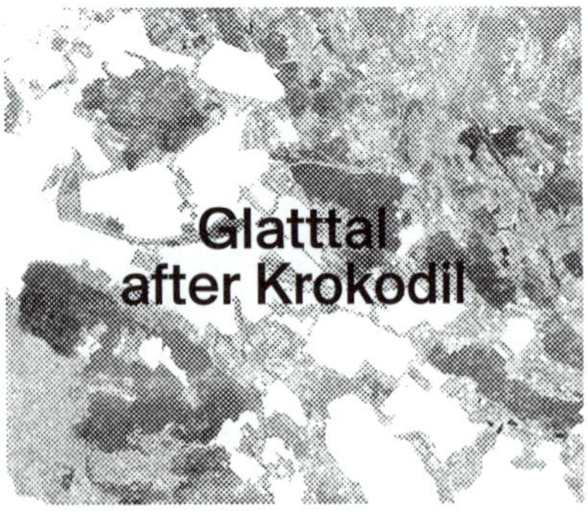

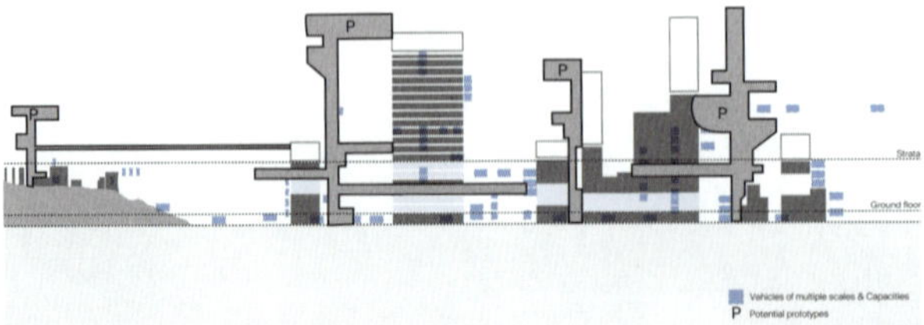

Guideline 1 Customize mobility

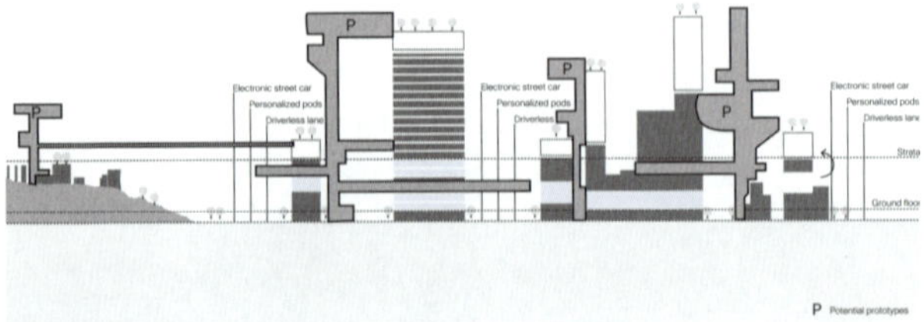

Guideline 2 Relieve ground floor space

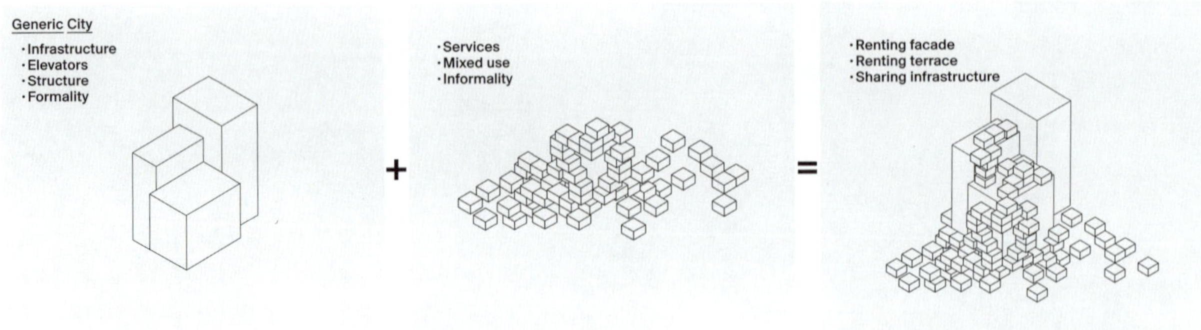

Fractal-Space-Connector

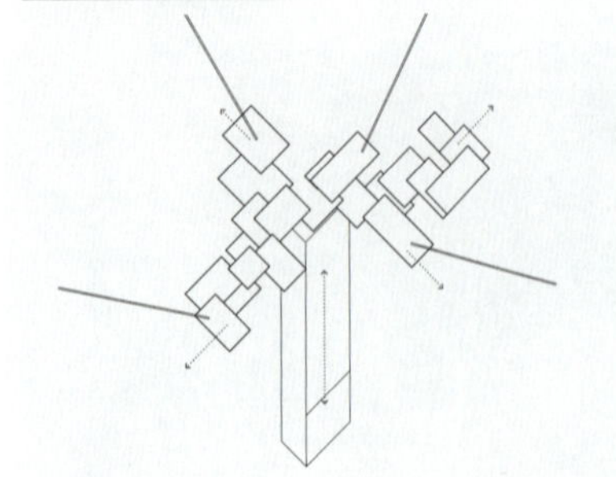

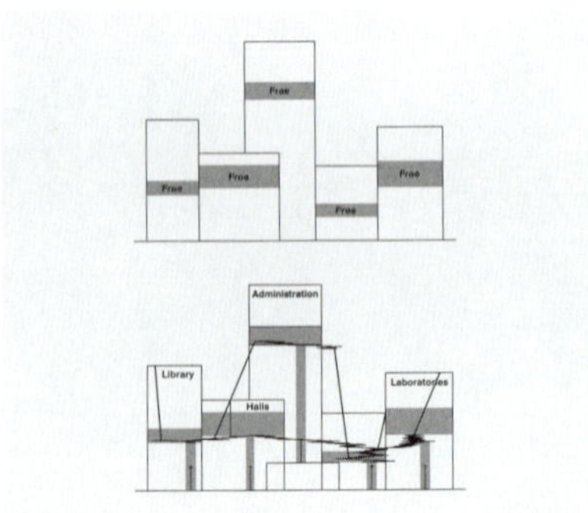

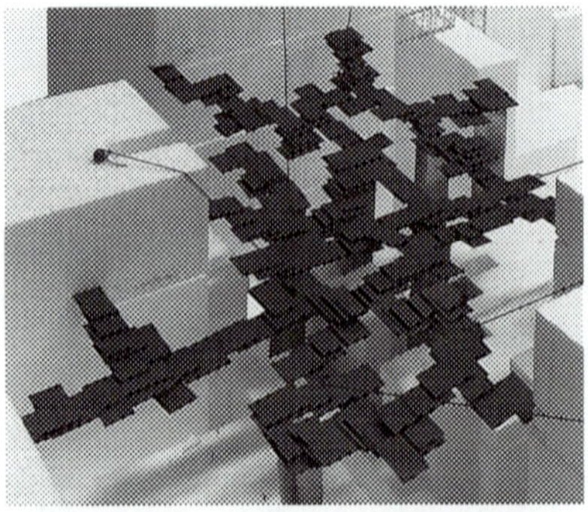

Up-side-down

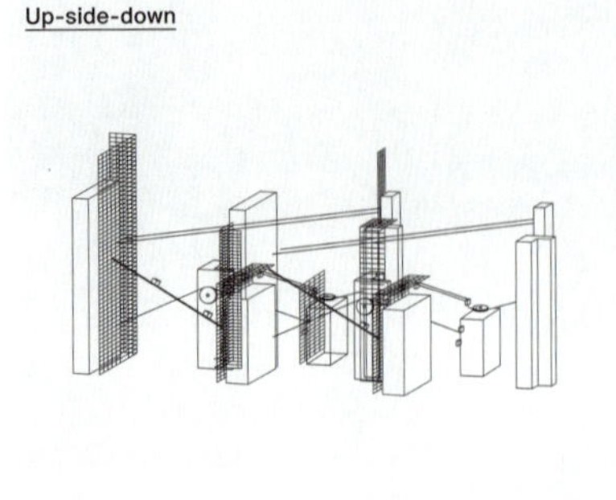

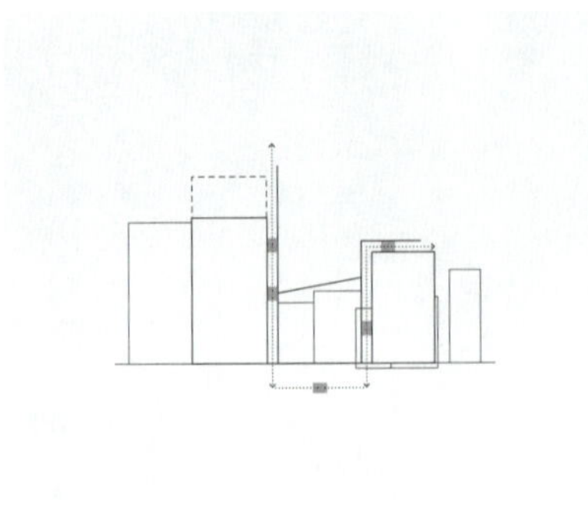

- Top Down
- Planned
- Axial
- Formal
- Dictatorial

- Grid
- Inflexible
- Centralized
- Predefined
- Divided

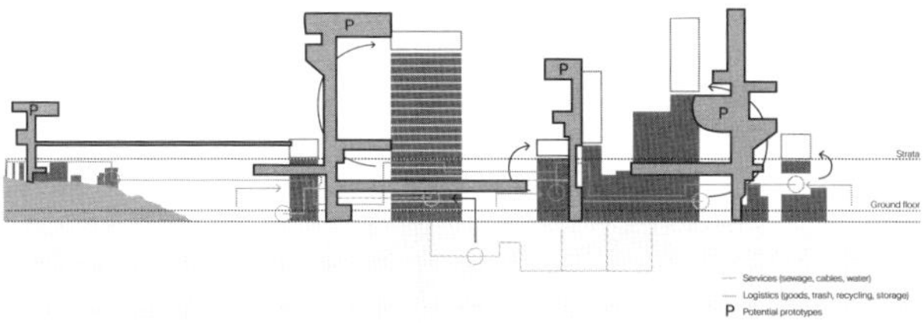

Guideline 3 Relocate services and logistics

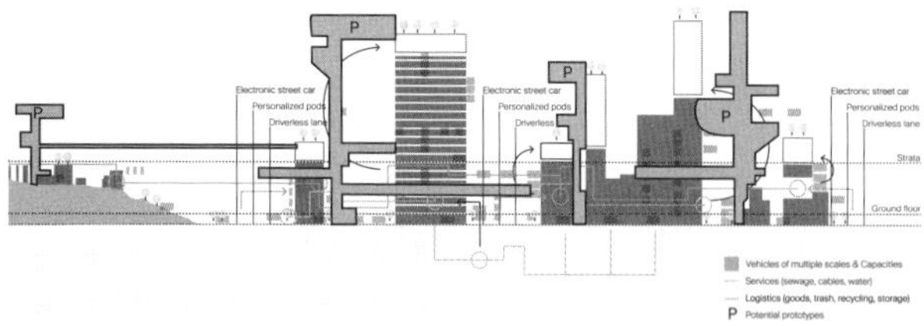

Strategic Guidelines Customize mobility, relocate services and logistics, relieve ground floor space

Flexible and Temporary City

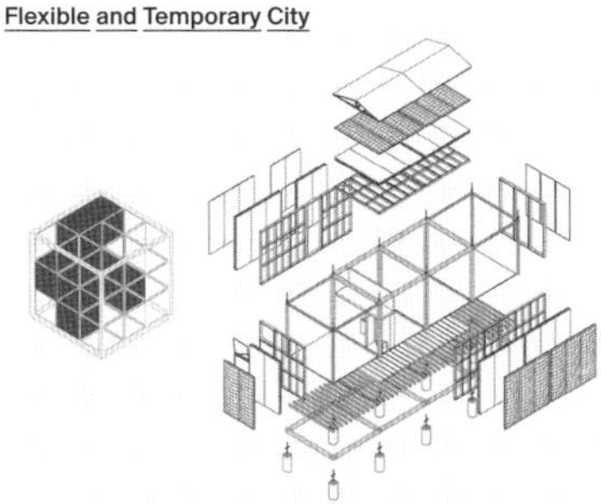

The Loop

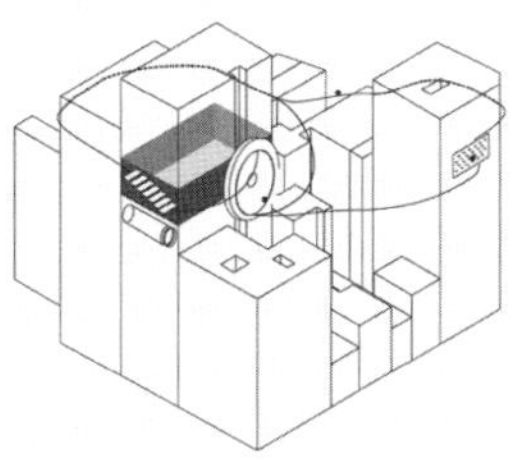

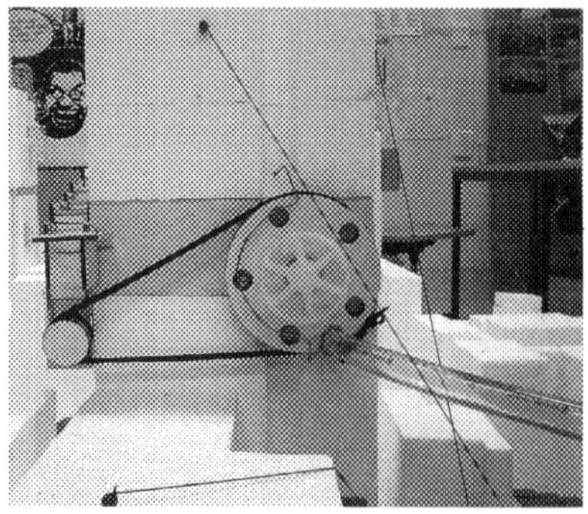

Caterpillar

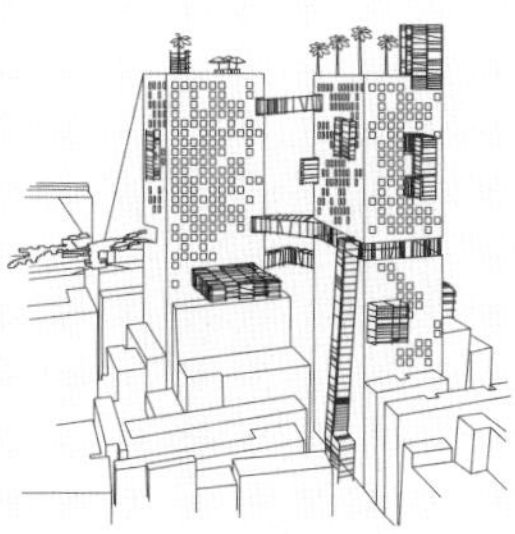

Recycle and Produce—Efficent Roofscapes

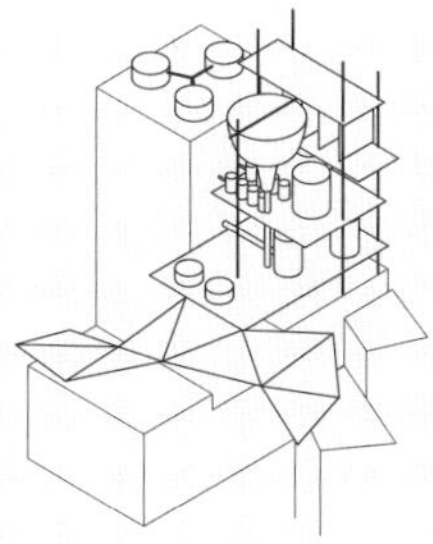

New City (Continous, Constant Movement)

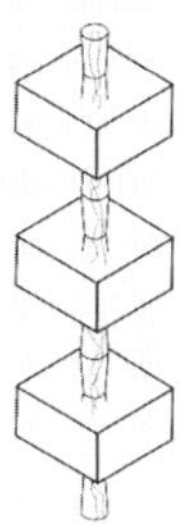

Rooftop Connection

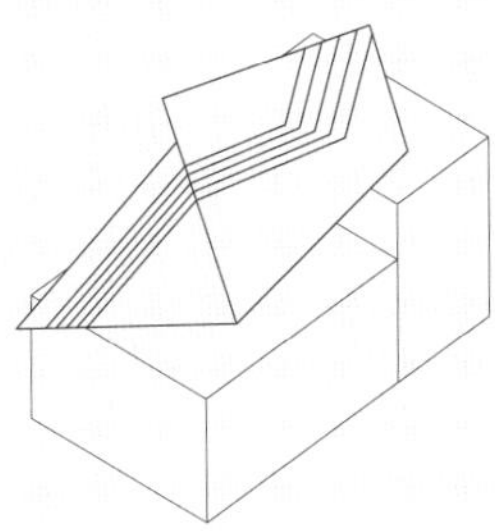

Studio F
Lecturer Kunlé Adeyemi
Assistant Monica Velasco
Students Ourania Argeiti, Nadine Coetzee, Marie-Annick Horton, Johanna Joecker, Rita Natascha Naidu, Caroline Oehler, Fabien Oulevay, Brian Owens-Murphy, Gunnar Ploner, Julie Riis Andersen, Richard Seymour, Stefan Welter

As part of the *International Summer Academy*, Studio F explored *mobility in developing cities*. With the increasingly global focus on economic development, social development, and environmental protection, the conceptual framework for mobility in Glatttal was conceived through the lens of "developing cities" as a practical basis for understanding urban transformations.

The studio investigated various forms of mobility on land, water, and air. It revisited history, analyzed the present, and projected the future of an upwardly mobile, urban environment for Glatttal city. The areas focused on were: Curitiba, Lagos, and Mumbai.

The first step in the studio work was a site study of Glatttal followed by documentation of the results. After acquiring an understanding of the urban, economical, spatial, and social impacts of mobility, the studio created conceptual mappings and collages of mobility modes in Glatttal to represent current and future urban transformations. Mobility was seen as an urban catalyst, densifier, and transformer.

A taste of Curitiba in Schwerzenbach

Mobility in Developing Cities

An urban intervention in mobility, which addresses the challenges of developing the city Glatt, at the same time, harnesses its rich social, environmental and infrastructural potentials.

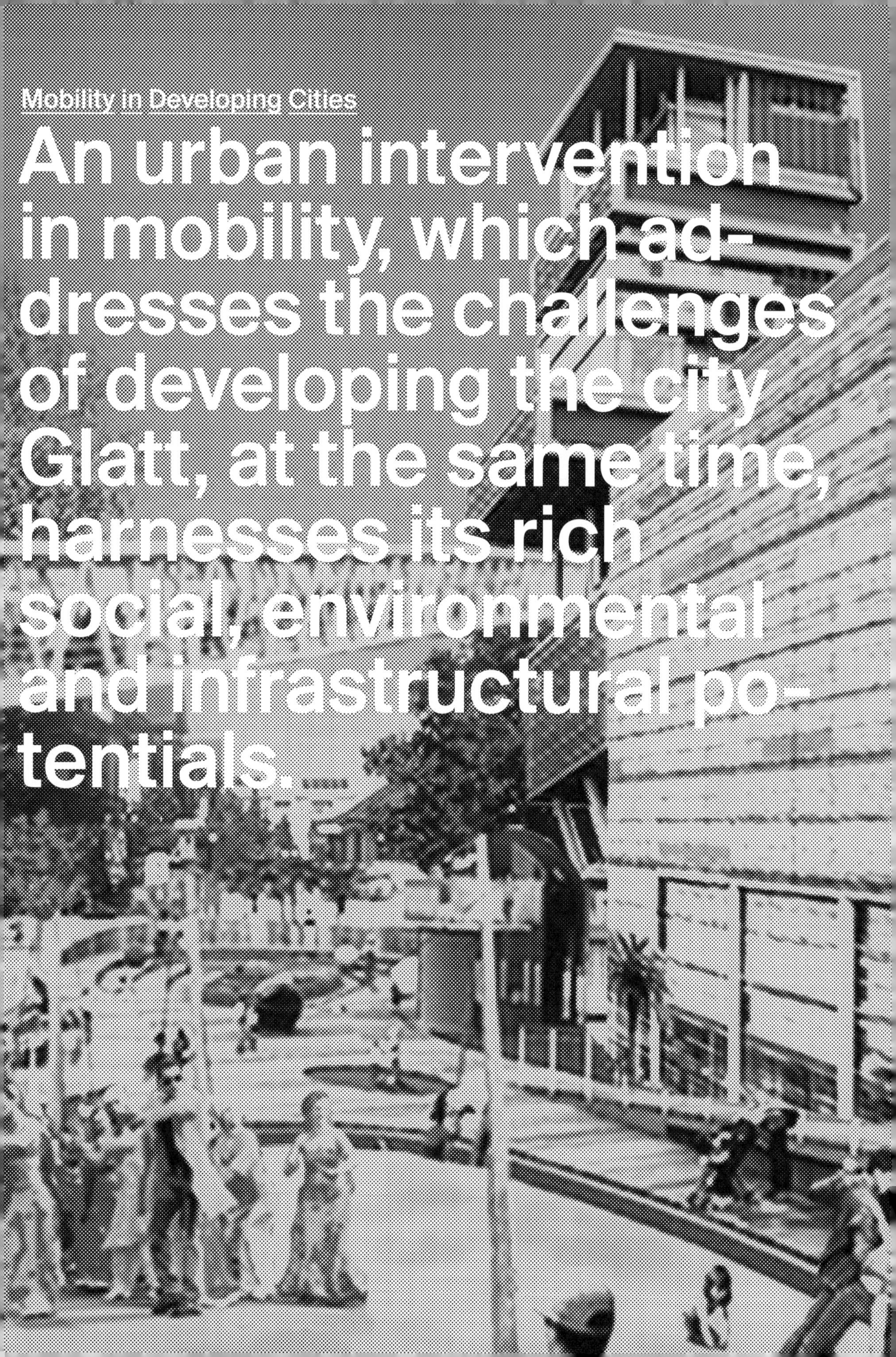

Slow mobility in Dübendorf

Recreational spots transferred from Mumbai to Wangen-Brüttisellen

Case Study of the Area Focussed on

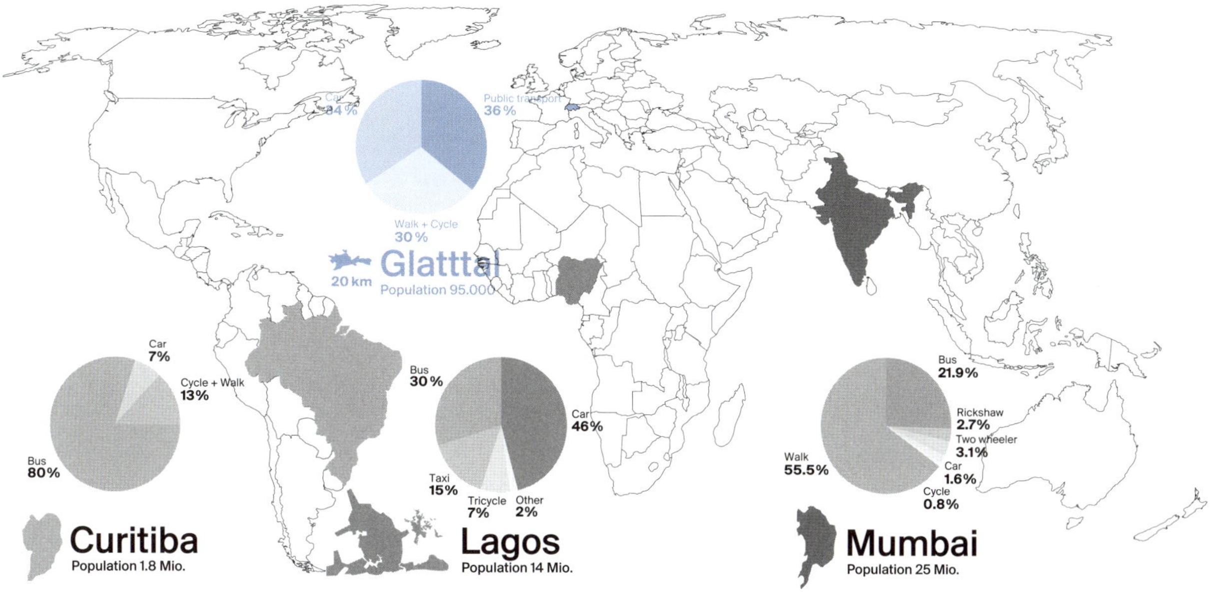

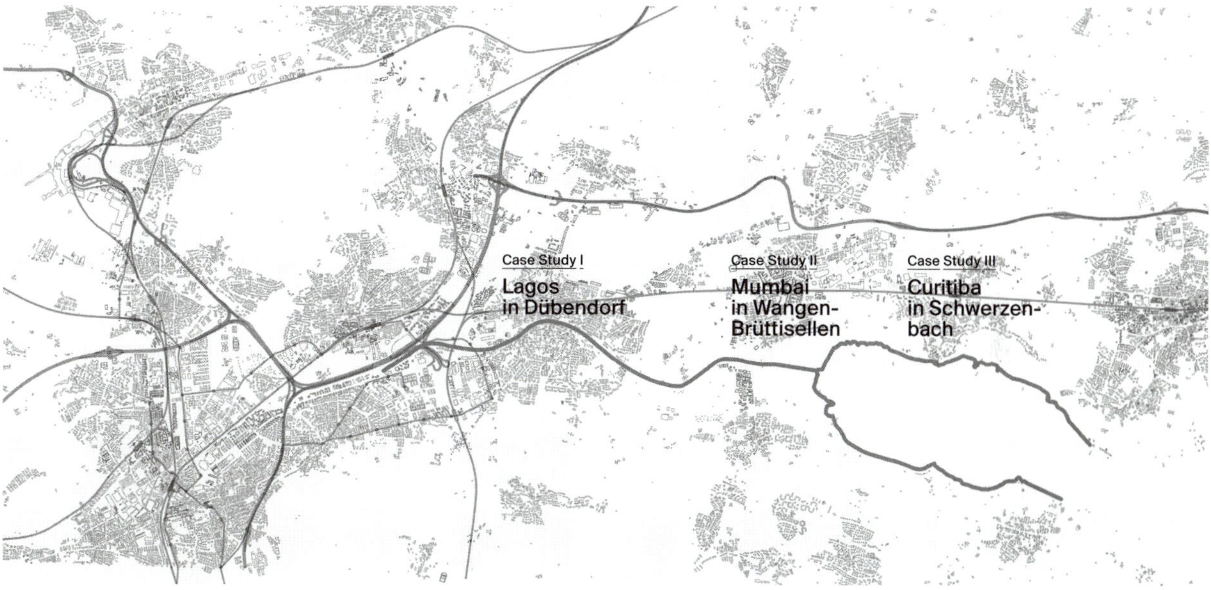

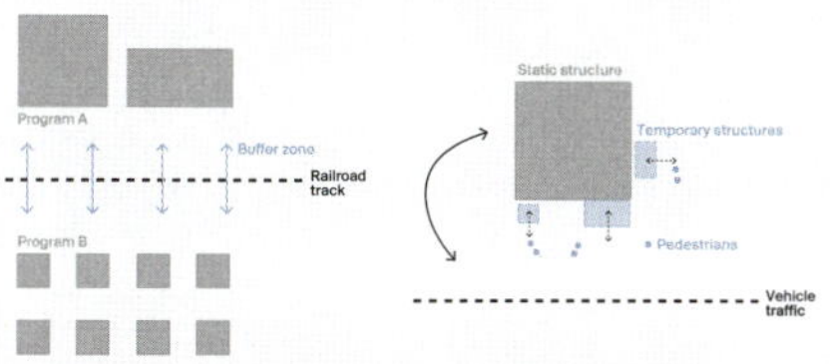

Buffer between contrasting programs

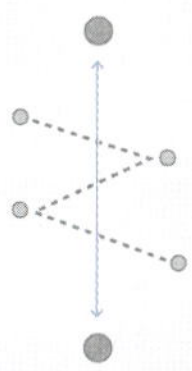

Global links / Local thresholds

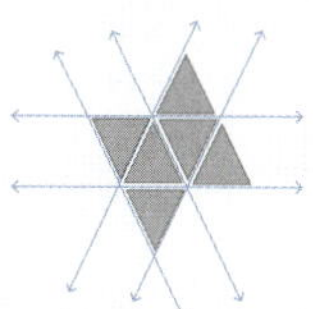

Slicing the landscape

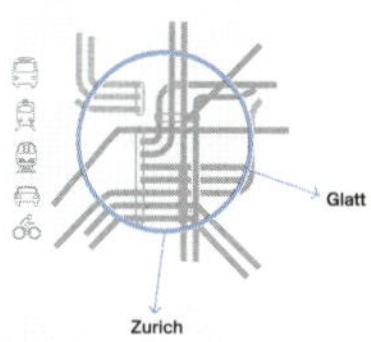

Transportation hubs

The reason is that the landscape is less contaminated, or at least less ideologically suspect, than the built form.

Architects Group Krokodil

Landscape

Landscape is one of the most powerful design tools in urban planning. This has been the case since the clear separation between town and landscape was abolished in the Baroque era, and, naturally, to an even greater extent as a consequence of present-day suburbanization processes in which the city expands into the landscape. Beyond a certain size, overriding urban landscapes can be made legible only by means of landscape design.

Henry Le Notre's garden in Versailles reflected the way in which the *roi soleil* saw himself by intervening spatially in the landscape and subduing it, while in the process also extending the rooms of the palace into the landscape. With his Central Park in New York, *Frederick Law Olmsted* created the exemplary model of landscape in the city. A rectangular piece of Manhattan is omitted from the urbanization process. A park landscape is used to create an alternative to the pulsating metropolis. By means of the contrast, both city and park are further heightened. *Peter Bredsdorff's* Finger Plan for Copenhagen regulates the growth of the metropolis and interlocks built-up districts with the green areas between them. Green recreation areas are created between the development axes. Green spaces and urban areas determine each other, each giving the other its form.

Under the generic term Landscaping, Studio I, *Flughafen Park*, Studio J, *Scales of Water*, and Studio B, *We Love Suburbia*, deal with the question of what landscape means for the present-day city. How do the city and landscape engage one another? Do they determine or penetrate each other? Does one alter the other? What do landscape and agriculture mean in the city? Is landscape infrastructure in the sense of transport space, meeting space, and recreation space? Can landscape make city out of the periphery?

Public architecture and public spaces can create social and economic arenas that promote long-term, community-based policies and urban renewal.
Alfredo Brillembourg & Hubert Klumpner

What kinds of technologies and infrastructures are needed to respond to the varied demands of urban open space?
Martin Rein-Cano

How has the crisis of ownership in our time changed the general perception of private vs. public (shared) space?
Martin Rein-Cano

How do advances in communication, mobility, and clothing inform requirements for open spaces?
Martin Rein-Cano

... The transformation of a central landscape zone into a park structuring the future city development of Glatttal.
Christophe Girot & Lukas Schweingruber

Studio I
Lecturer Martin Rein-Cano
Assistant Anouk Kuitenbrouwer
Students Johanna Backhaus, Joël Béla Bourgeois, Martin Dumont, Yael Liebetrau, Kobe Macco, Alice Matos de Pina, Sandra Misteli, Nicole Theresa Raab, Mario Andres Vahos Moreno, Stefan Serafin Weber, Shenghua Yan, Léonard Ziegler

Open space has lost many of its conventions. What used to be defined as *free space*, where there was no specific, defined program and private and public functions were clearly distinguished, has seen its borders softened. The decisions of an urban master plan and the consequent permanence of even the most frivolous item of architecture are incompatible with the instability of the metropolis. Metropolitan suburban agglomerations can be seen as the current dominant type of spatial organization, with the typical traits of the *Zwischenstadt*—urbanized areas without any aesthetic appeal—of which the Glatttal region is a good example. This diagnosis calls, in turn, for a more specific design and the concept of landscape is the only one capable of integrating heterogeneous structures on the level of perception. An aesthetic approach to urbanized areas is mandatory.

The studio therefore aimed at identifying a possible actor or site with the potential to stimulate the further development of the city of Kloten. The proximity to Zurich Airport presented itself as a possible generator of a new urbanity: like the railway station in the nineteenth century, the airport can be understood as the new starting point of urban development. Zurich Airport is a major European gateway; 17 million travelers use the complex every year and change airplanes for intercontinental flights. The airport dynamics can intervene in the urban reality of Kloten in a positive way; a common open space would allow a mutual influence and provide a currently lacking leisure environment for both travelers and inhabitants of its surroundings. Adopting a park as the first step in a city's development—much like the role played by Central Park in the subsequent settlement of New York's urban tissue—secures its quality as open space. The airport park can thus be seen as the new gateway to the city.

The project proposes a strategy that—by combining programmatic diversity with design specificity—will generate a new kind of open space. Two existing hills are shaped in a clearly man-made landscape where the major programmatic components are distributed on the different levels of the park, so that ambiances remain similar on each level but can quickly change with vertical displacement. A new typology of open spaces is defined by appropriating the airport's infrastructure, generating three kinds of mobility: standard park pathways, a vertical sequence of escalators, and the "*people-mover*," promoting a mechanical *promenade* through the lower levels of the park. Programmatic connections and a subversive reinterpretation of the classical image of the garden produce a completely standard open space. A *machine-like* park that—like in a theater—offers the illusion of open space: sublimity and dreams, substances for the soul.

Flughafen Park

A major theme will be how the integration of technology and infra-structure can allow for alternative spaces to the traditional workplace that make productive activities feasible out-doors.

Birds-eye View of Flughafen Park

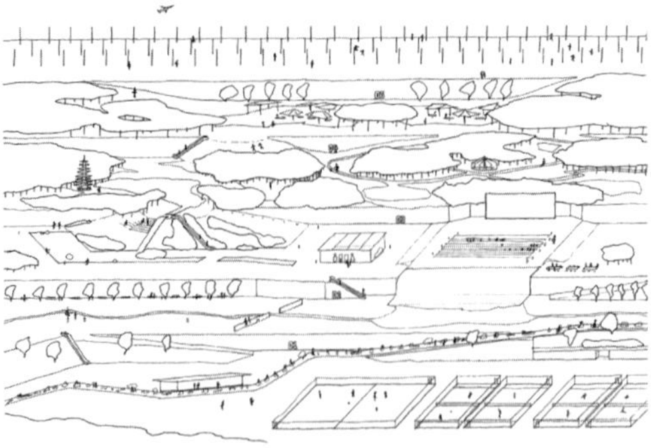

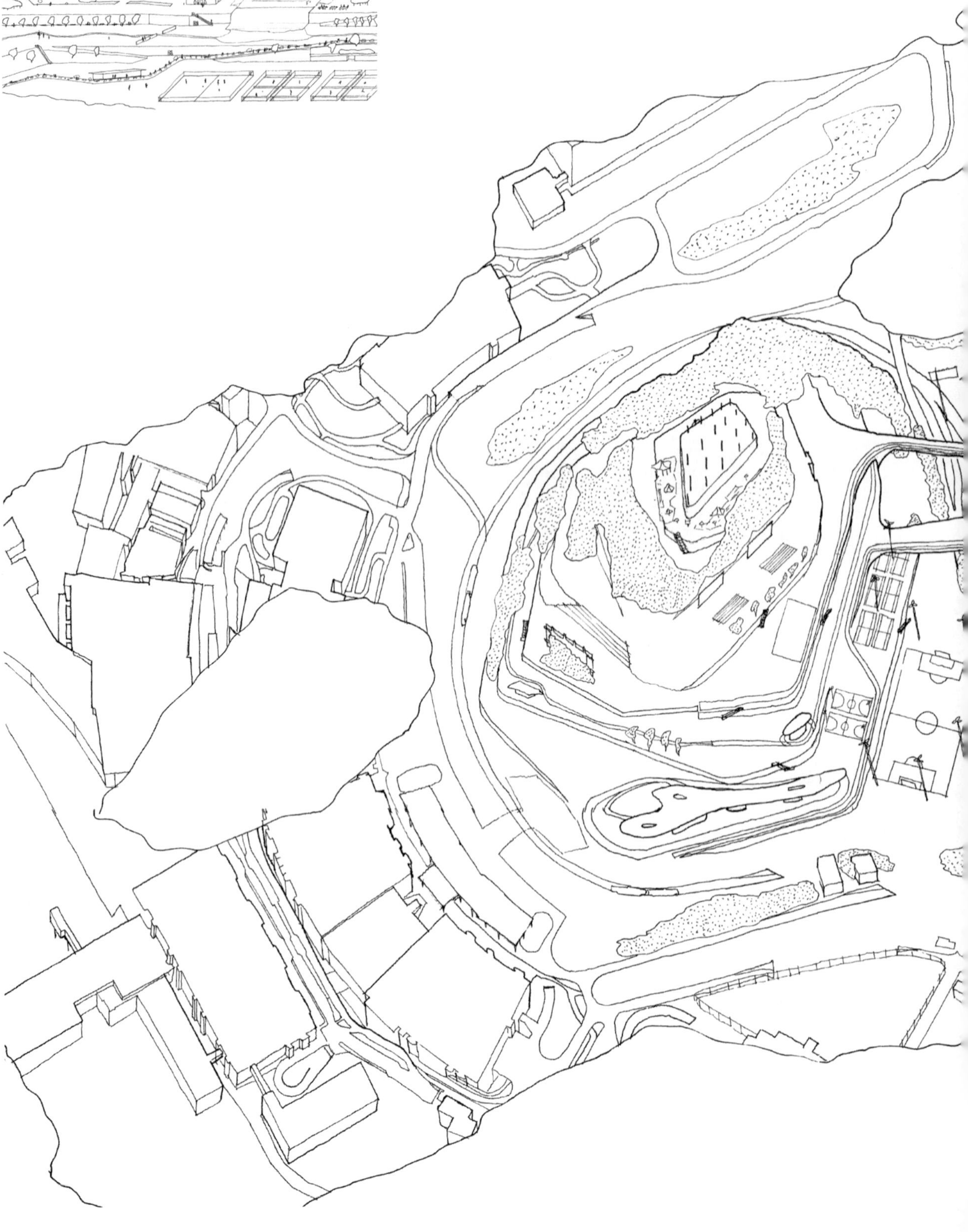

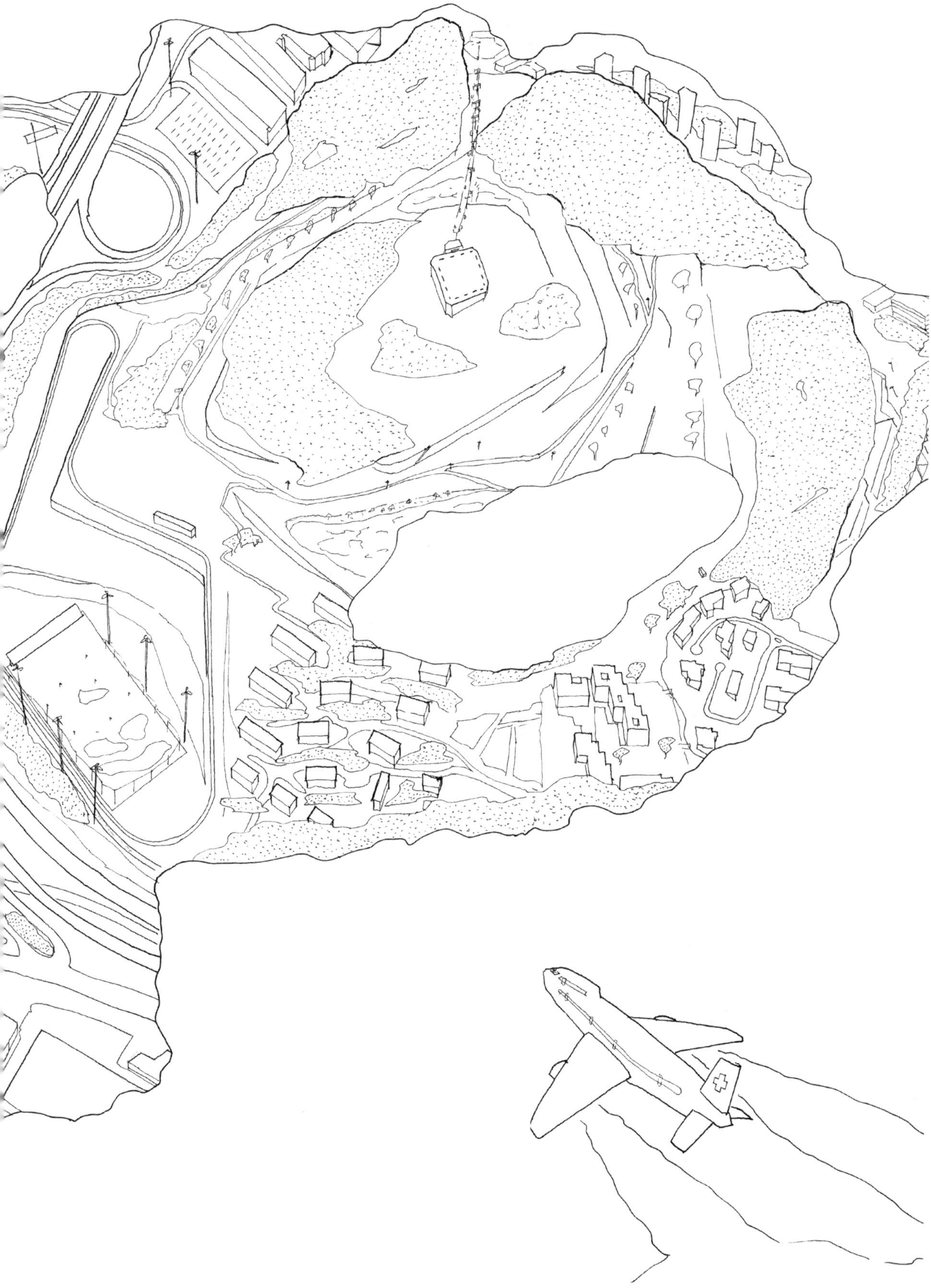

Entrance

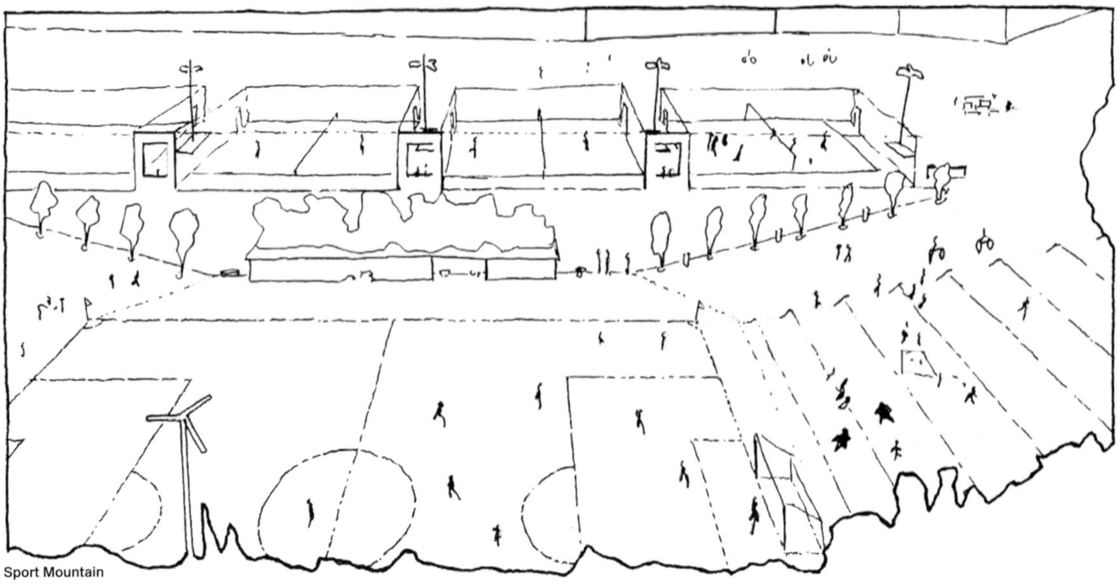

Sport Mountain

Entertainment, movies

Bridges

Sport Mountain

Vertical movement is enabled by escalators

Studio J
Lecturers Christophe Girot, Lukas Schweingruber
Assistants Dominik Bückers, Ilmar Hurxens, James Melsom
Students Elena Chestnova, Maxime Cloarec, Li Ran, Ruizhe Liang, Georgios Orfanopoulos, Melissa Pestalozzi, Styliani Rossikopoulou-Pappa, Lorenzo Santosuosso, Tiia Vahula, Rosanne Weijers, Karen Wong, Francesca Zorat

Today, the Glatt River occupies only a fraction of the valley floor that it once dominated. From the beginning of the nineteenth century, the valley's meandering rivers and swamps began disappearing into channels and culverts. The utilitarian goal of these infrastructures ignored the natural landscape and prepared the valley for unrestrained urbanization structured only by colorful zoning plans. The villages occupying the Glatttal have since expanded to form an almost continuous carpet of dwellings, industrial areas, and office parks. Landscape structure, local identity, and urban spaces lack quality and cohesion.

By acknowledging the inherent quality of the Glatt River as the backbone of the valley and activator of urban life, "Scales of Water" focused on seven different areas in the valley, each of which were identified by their own distinctive qualities: infrastructure, agriculture, city, nature, leisure, culture, and sport. By starting with an analysis of the topography and water system it was possible to gain a precise understanding of the structure of the valley. Following the diverse nature of the Glatttal today, the natural landscape was just as much a starting point for the design studio as man-made infrastructures, such as highways and water channels.

With the help of CNC milling and model projections, the individual projects were collated to form a master plan that integrates the characteristic topography and urban structure of the Glatttal.

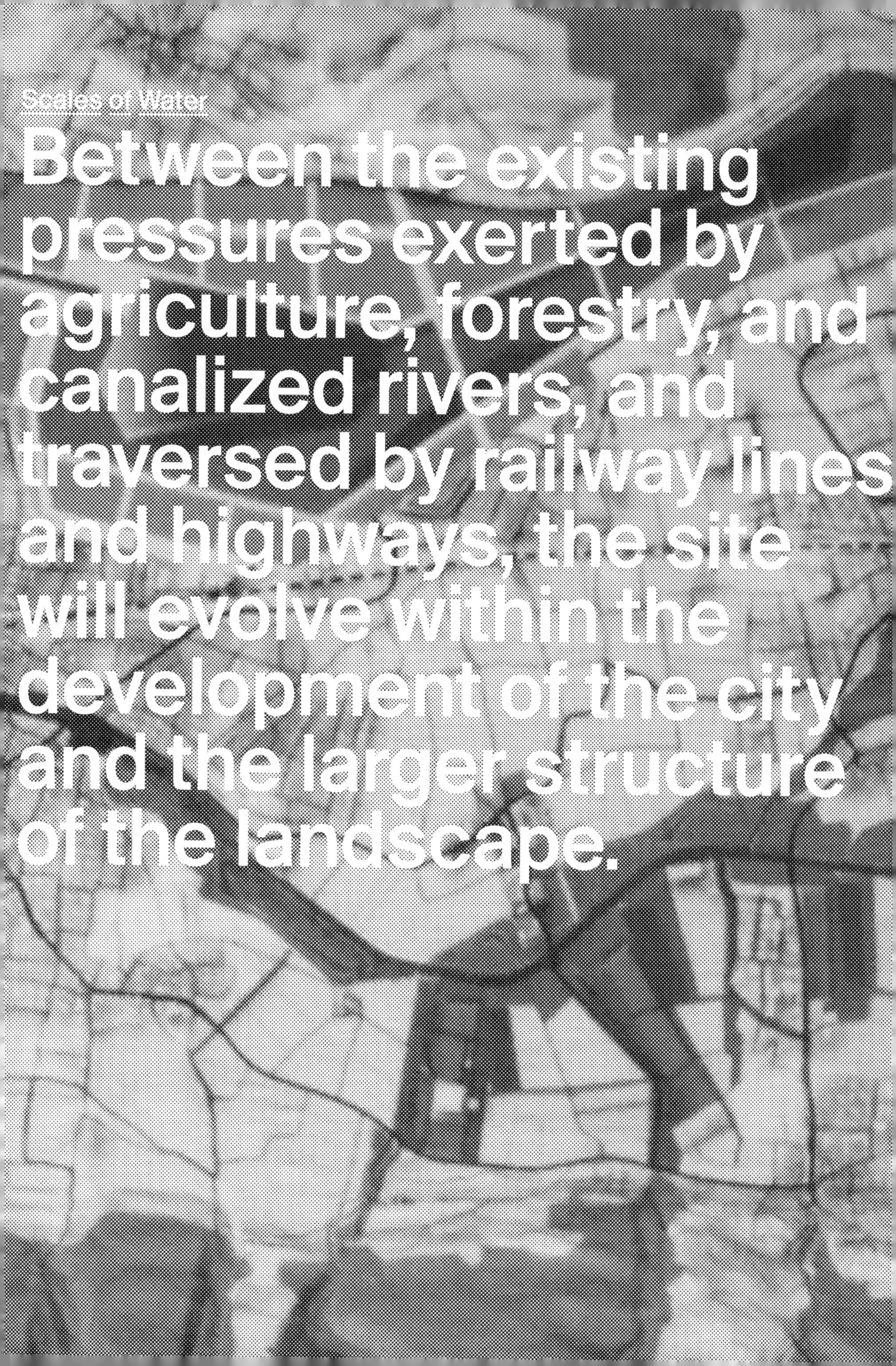

Scales of Water

Between the existing pressures exerted by agriculture, forestry, and canalized rivers, and traversed by railway lines and highways, the site will evolve within the development of the city and the larger structure of the landscape.

Water as History. Water as Identity

Water is the defining element in the Glatttal; winding rivers & swamps shaped the topographical landscape of the valley.

Water & Lost Identity

In recent history the water disappeared into channels and culverts. The Greifensee remains the sole structural water element.

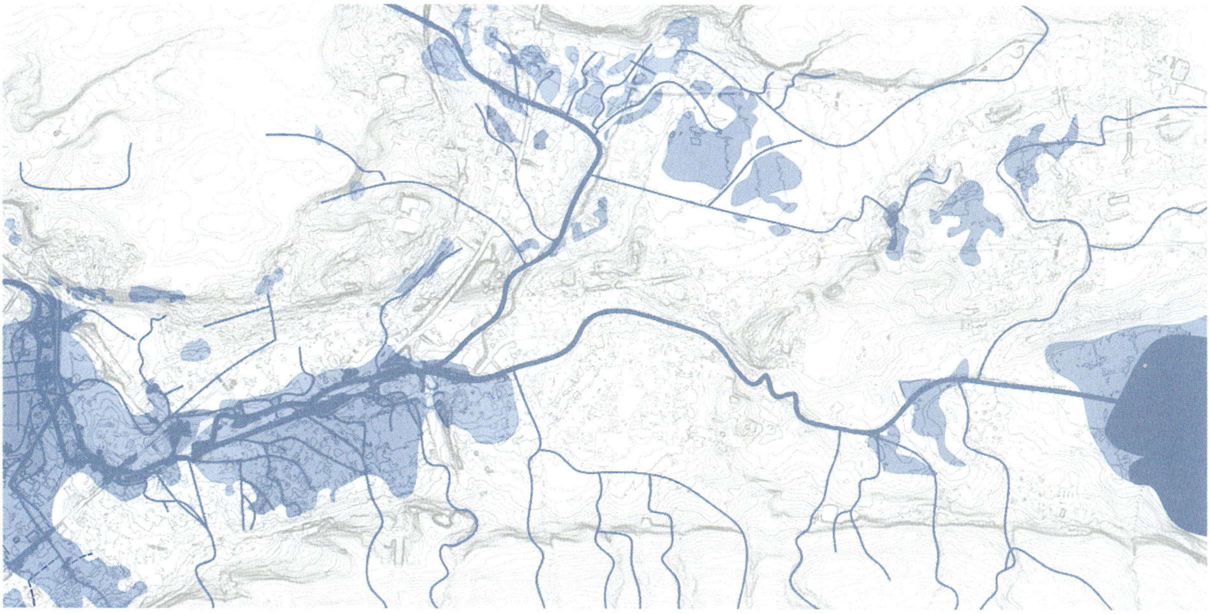

The Comeback?

What is the role of water in a future development of the Glatt-tal? Can water again be a determining factor adding identity and value to the site?

Water as an Amplifier

Water appears in different forms, scales, and uses with its surrounding uses. Together with water, existing identities are emphasized, new individual identities are created.

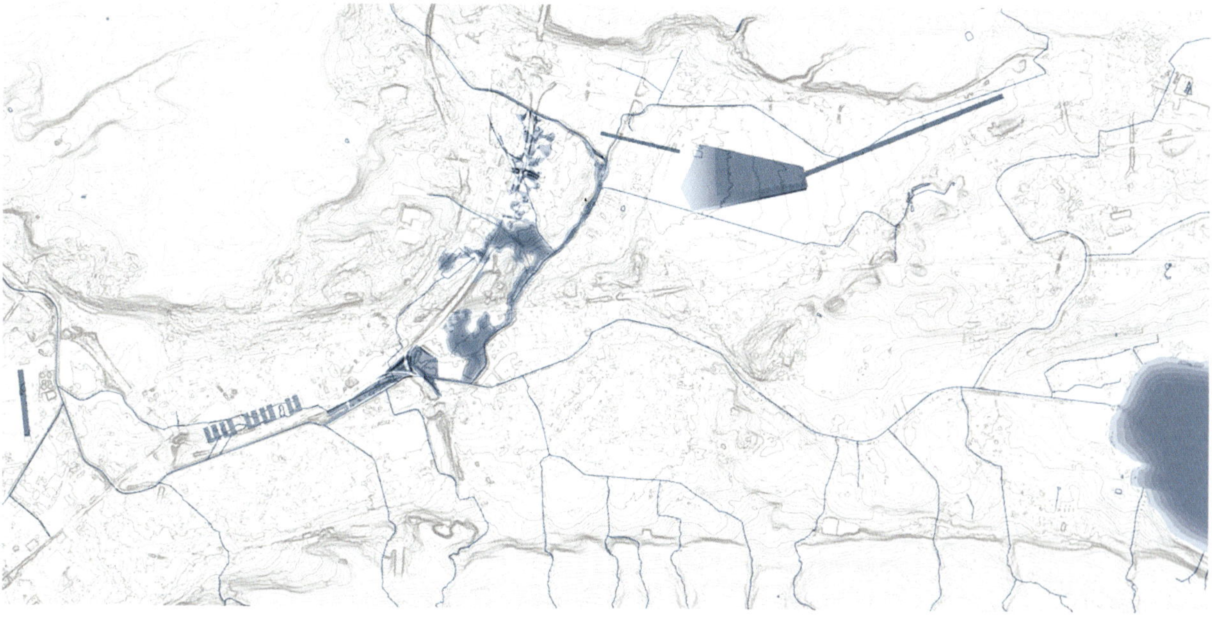

Studio B
Lecturer Don Murphy
Assistant Shaya Fallahi
Students Tugce Doyuran, Ignacio Frade Roldán, Cédric Gwenaël Gil, Farah Kassab, Elena Khasyanova, Natalia Milerska, Jaqueline Reiser, Flavio Schnelli

The urban discourse divides the built environment into three clear categories: urban, suburban, and rural. Glatt is suburban, a region on the periphery of the city of Zurich. However, on the site, one immediately notes the peculiar juxtaposition of a farm, office building, and detached houses. As architects, we often dismiss this suburban condition as a "bad urban situation"; hence the reaction often is to make a "Stadt" (a city). The team could clearly read this attempt in the master plan presented by the Krokodil Group. Rather than repeating the exercise with another reactionary plan for the current condition; our point of entry begins by acknowledging Swiss suburbia.

In making suburbia there are two key aspects that allow for urban sprawl. First, it requires an expanding infrastructure network, second, the availability of an expansive natural landscape. The lack of a tradition and history of urban planning practice in Switzerland offers us an opportunity to revisit the current global approach to city-making that is being employed in Zurich today. Switzerland can boast a well connected infrastructure network of roads, railways, and tunnels. Therefore, rather than imposing an anonymous city plan on the landscape (Krokodil master plan proposal); the density of the development becomes key in making use of the strong connectivity, while maintaining and utilizing the Swiss landscape.

The initial key to resolving urban sprawl is to revisit the scale of the suburban city and build settlements of appropriate density. Mixed program functions can be integrated in the landscape, rather than being laid out in a *tabula rasa*. The analogy of the tip of the iceberg was observed repeatedly in certain local projects that were analysed and seen as Swiss solutions that allow for mixed-use activity and density in compact forms, such as Zurich Main Station.

Using the geographical understanding of coast that relates to the sea; the team revisited the city edge by drawing a suggestive coast around Glatt. This suggested a new reading of a suburban landscape which was previously considered as monotonous.

As an example, three key sites were selected that offer different coastal conditions; the bay, the beach and the cliff. The edge condition was analyzed to determine different densities and orientations across the three sites.

Zurich's political dynamic can be seen as a hindrance for new rapid and effective change, as, in order for action to be taken, it requires the collective consensus of individuals. We believe that, having based the intent of the development on people's aspirations, we can define a political front that is agreed upon by the general public.

In conclusion, the approach taken to suburbia is not to eliminate it by making a second city, but rather to enhance its qualities in a way that responds to the needs of urban living. Capitalizing on the natural landscape by carefully defining urban growth boundaries, a variety of contexts will govern the development process. This will stimulate new functional and formal interventions that will define the contemporary identity of the North Coast which can serve as a synonym for the Swiss urban model.

We Love Suburbia

… Architects see very few qualities in the suburban environment.

Extractions

Island

Coast

Infrastructure

The Swiss Solution

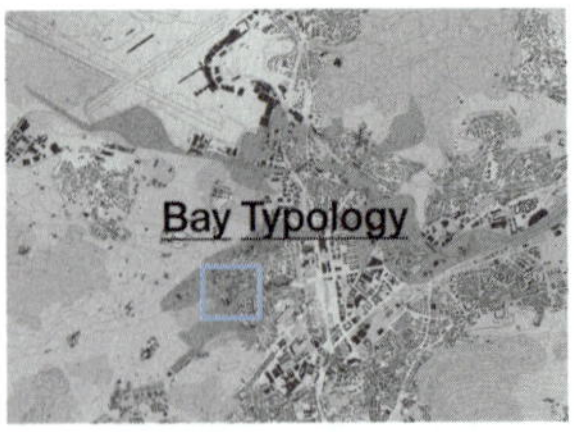

Study area A

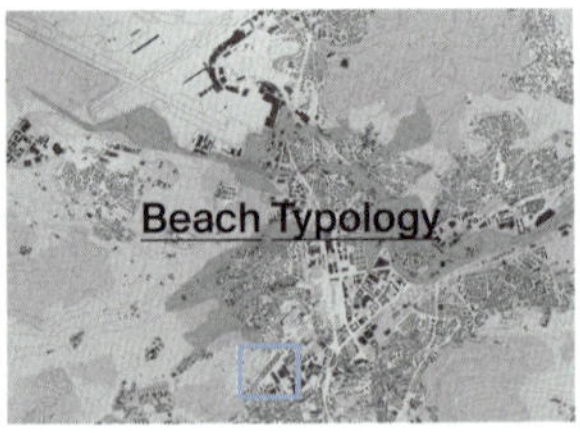

Study area B

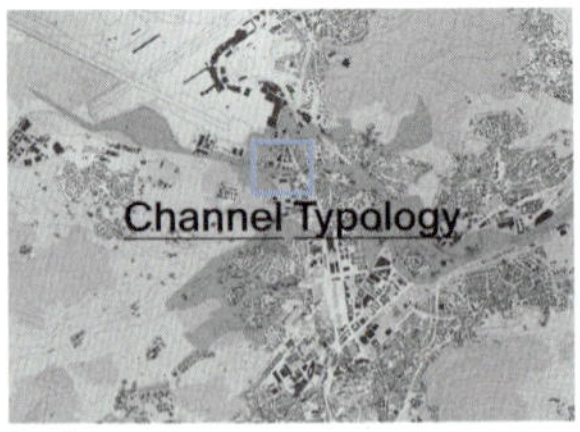

Study area C

Existing situation

Existing situation

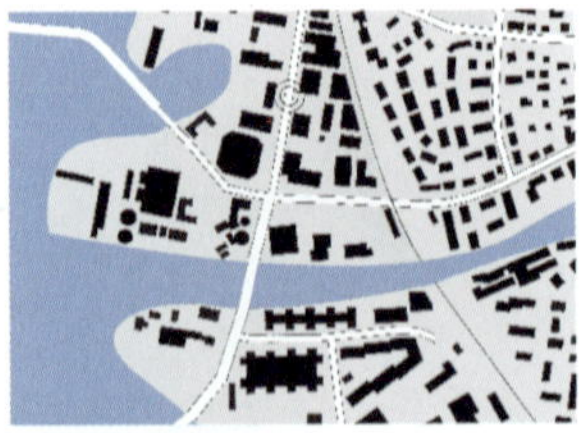

Existing situation

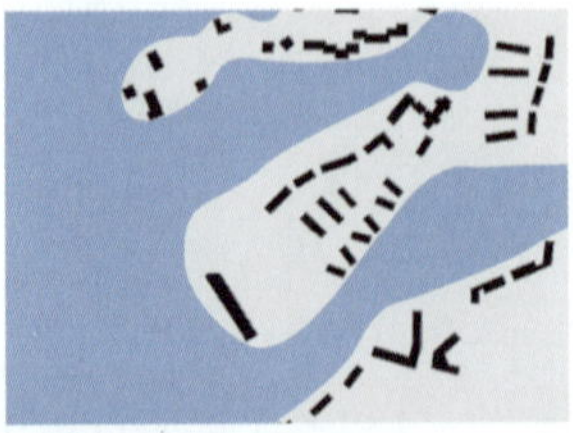

Step 1: Clean up

Step 1: Open up buildings to the beach

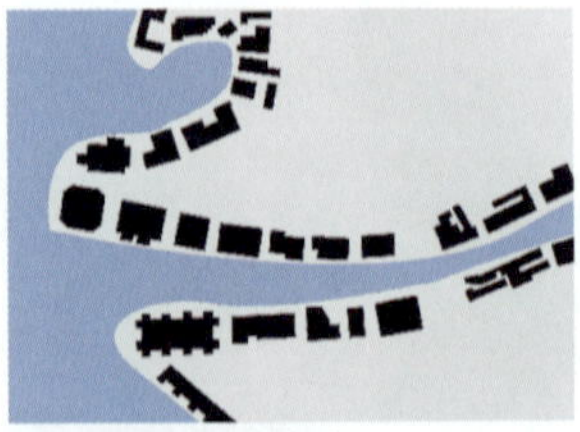

Step 1: High-rise at the shore

Step 2: Adding new buildings

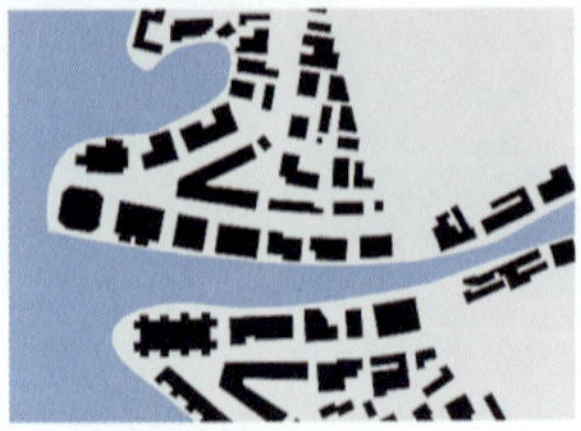

Step 2: Adding mid-rise

Step 3: Adding low-rise

Step 4: Adding transport system

Glatttal Coast

The North Coast

Hiding the infrastructure

Removing the commune boundaries

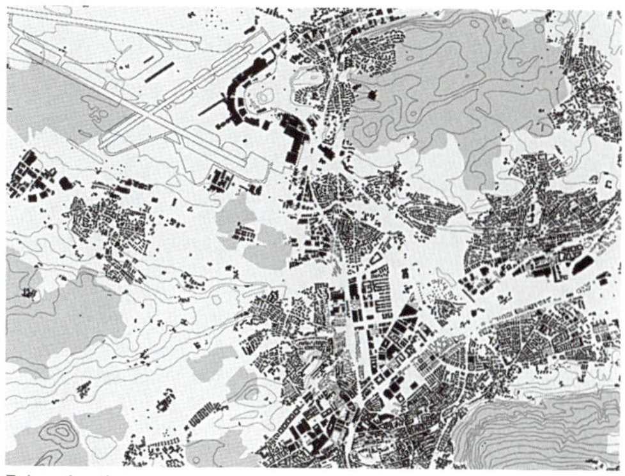

Enhancing the green

Defining the edge

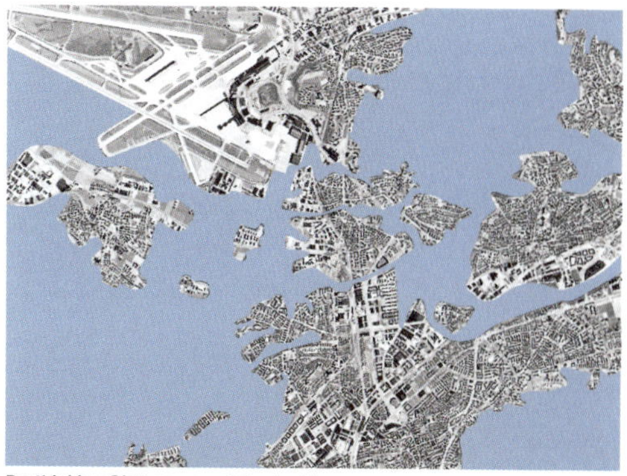

Re-thinking Glatt as a coastal suburbia

Glatttal is a polycentric urban landscape built up of existing elements and new, carefully positioned parts. But what is the concrete form, the model of this new city?

Architects Group Krokodil

Really increasing density would require a concept of the city that often finds confinement and concentration more exciting than airiness and expansiveness.

Marcel Meili

Given the predominance of landscape as both a spatial quality and an identity within the Landscape Park area of the Glatttal, the studio will propose the development of a series of “Island Subcities” as a strategy for organizing the future growth of the area.

Mark Lee

... How we can develop new typologies that could fulfill some of the desires of the general public, yet propose higher densities and possibilities for interaction, such as hybrid buildings with many functions ...

Don Murphy

Can our interventions be permanent and temporary at the same time, a building and a park, an infrastructure and an interior?

Boštjan Vuga

Deploying an acupuncture-logic of development of intensely defined zones, “Island subcities,” forwards an urban strategy for simultaneous preservation and development.

Mark Lee

The issue is who can be the author of the “form of the metropolitan region.”

Marcel Meili

Studio C
Lecturer Boštjan Vuga
Assistant Miha Čebulj
Students Maria Abadia Suanzes-Carpegna, Anny Ninoska Batista, Pedro Bernardo Dias, Ilke Deniz, Kaspar Fischer, Kasia Osiecka, Nina Radosavljevic, Feyza Yagci

Autobahn Inhabited Bridges (AIBs) become a catalyst of future urban transformation in the Glatttal. These big, new, and slightly awkward structures span over the autobahn (highway), connecting the north and the south side along a 4.7 km strip of the autobahn A1 / A4 / E41 / E60. The AIBs act not only as connectors, they themselves become a destination. We go there to play, work, and socialize; we can live and stay above the autobahn. The AIBs alter our perception of and relationship to the autobahn; we consider this boring, but efficient infrastructure as architecture, as an object that can be designed, changed, and appreciated. Listen to the sound of autobahn! Have a room with a view of the autobahn! Feel the autobahn! Finally, the AIBs that span over the autobahn transform it; with the introduction of a public shuttle on two outer lanes of the autobahn connecting the AIBs, the autobahn turns first of all into a city motorway that then becomes a proper boulevard of the new Glatttal city.

There are four AIBs proposed by the studio. Since they are anchored to the very different conditions of their particular locations along the stretch of autobahn, they have different programs and uses; the four AIBs are spatially very different. As such, as new destinations for inhabitants, visitors, or just passers-by, they could become case studies for bridging over the new Glatttal Boulevard.

Autobahn Inhabited Bridges (AIB)

We are interested in how the AIBs, these large-scale architectural interventions, become triggers of and for future urban transformations.

Autobahn Resort

Interconnected bars create a structure that hovers above and is parallel to the autobahn. The rooms in the resort open with views to the autobahn. The bridge is anchored in the romantic woods on the northern side. A smooth transition is made between the green of nature and the autobahn. Visitors to the Glatttal are invited to stop and stay in the resort.

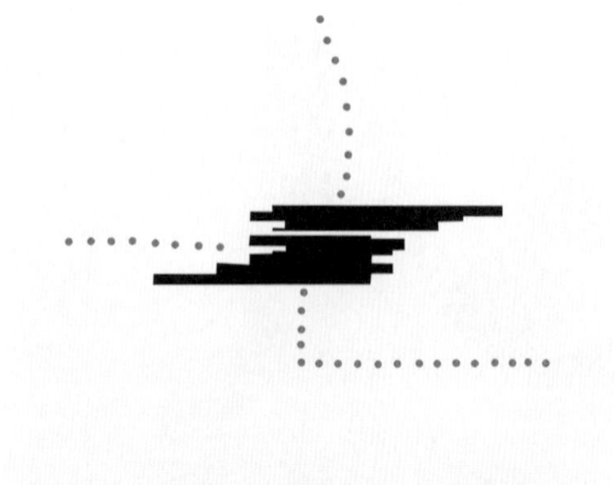

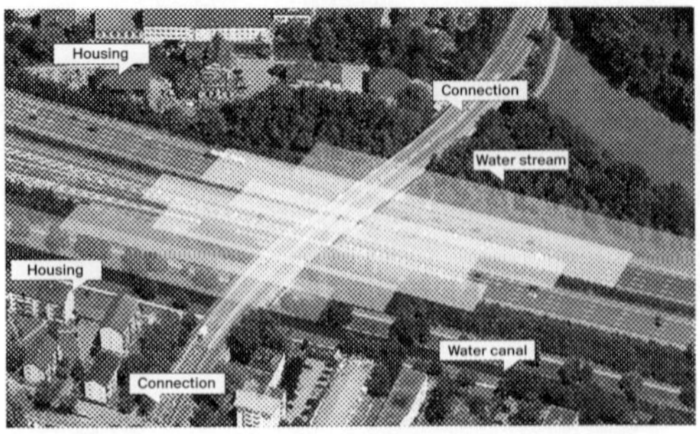

Health Plaza

A big floating platform is situated in the center of Glatttal, next to the shopping mall. A public plaza with health pavilions above the autobahn becomes a center of informal social activities in the Glatttal. You can even lie down and listen to the sound of the autobahn, channeled through pipes in the concrete.

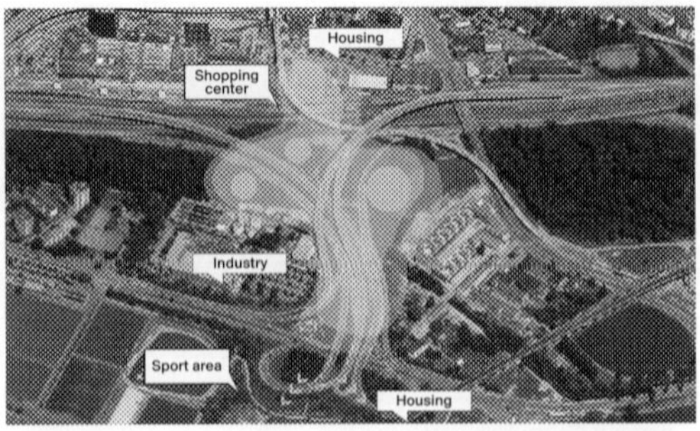

Adrenaline Farming

Two irregularly-shaped perforated slabs create an extension of fields and lawns over the autobahn. The upper slab covers a certain part of the lower one, creating interesting spatial conditions where people can plant greenery or vegetables and at the same time engage in sporting activities.

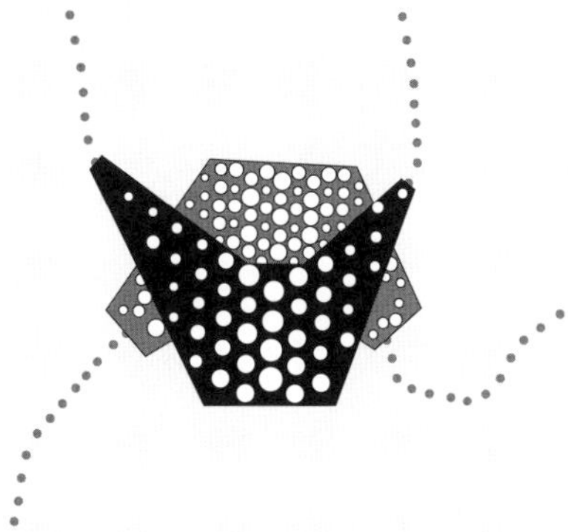

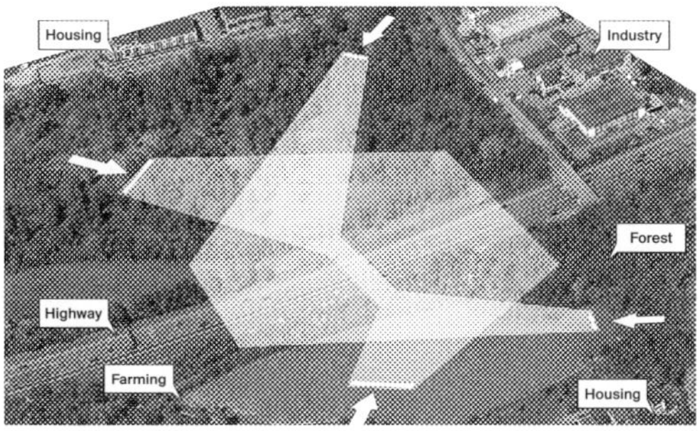

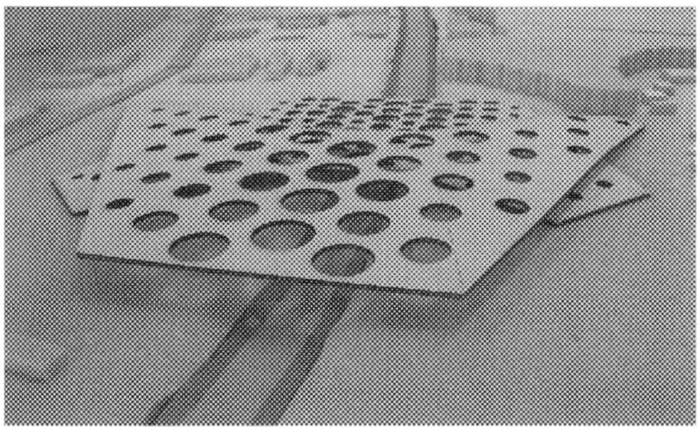

Vertical Village

Three mountainous towers rise from a public plaza above the autobahn. As such, they present a continuation of residential areas in the immediate surroundings. The task of the studio was the requalification of the autobahn through Glatttal. The four proposed bridges intensify the built structure of the suburban areas and trigger their transformation starting from the most fixed element: the autobahn.

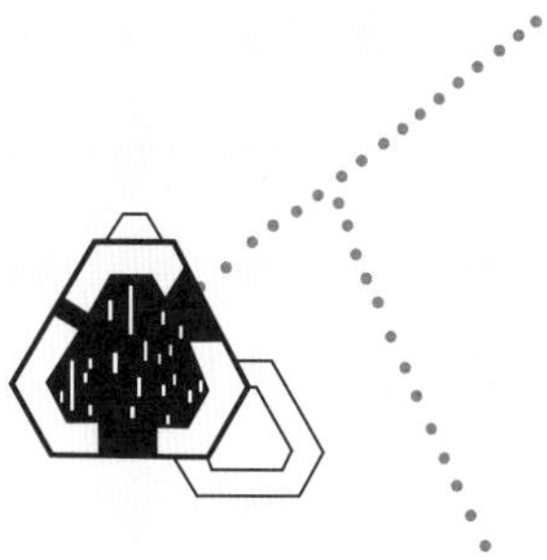

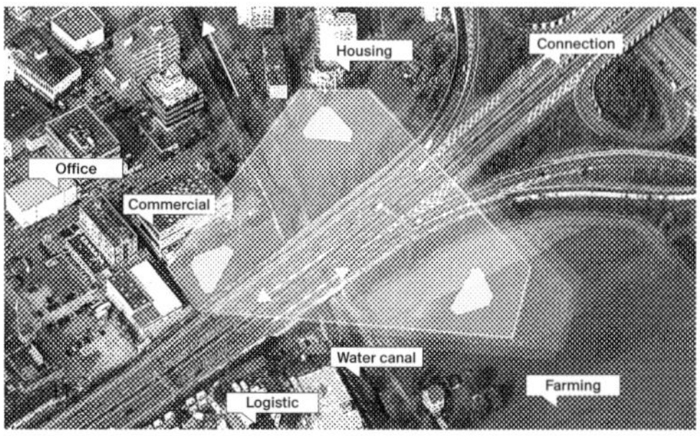

Studio H
Lecturer David Trottin
Students Phoebe Brady, Florentia Christoforou, Paulo Ricardo dos Santos Sousa, Viggo Fröst, Oana Andrea Grecea, Ian Watchorn, Iris Winkenbach, Alen Žunić

The aims of Krokodil's urban project for the Glatttal, to develop urban densification while trying to maintain a respectful relationship between landscape and the existing built environment, seemed very ambitious. The new master plan modified the city by inserting a collage of new blocks into landscape gaps between the existing sprawl. We regarded the desire to maintain intense landscape spaces or farming areas to connect urban communities as a particular strength of the proposal.

However, for us, the workshop theme *From Suburb to City* suggested a stronger relation towards urban intensity. This intensity is translated into an increase in the density of built-up areas and characteristic public spaces. Simultaneously, urban sprawl needs to be restricted in order to minimize transport systems and maintain land reserves for future generations. Also, the evolution towards more public transport and soft mobility dictates greater proximity and a new urban scheme with higher density. While retaining Krokodil's idea of collage, our studio therefore suggests a more radical focus for the project, assuming 100-percent city / 100-percent country.

Small Walled City

We need to carry out research on hybrid forms that can deal with such paradoxical urban typologies as the mega-building and the village.

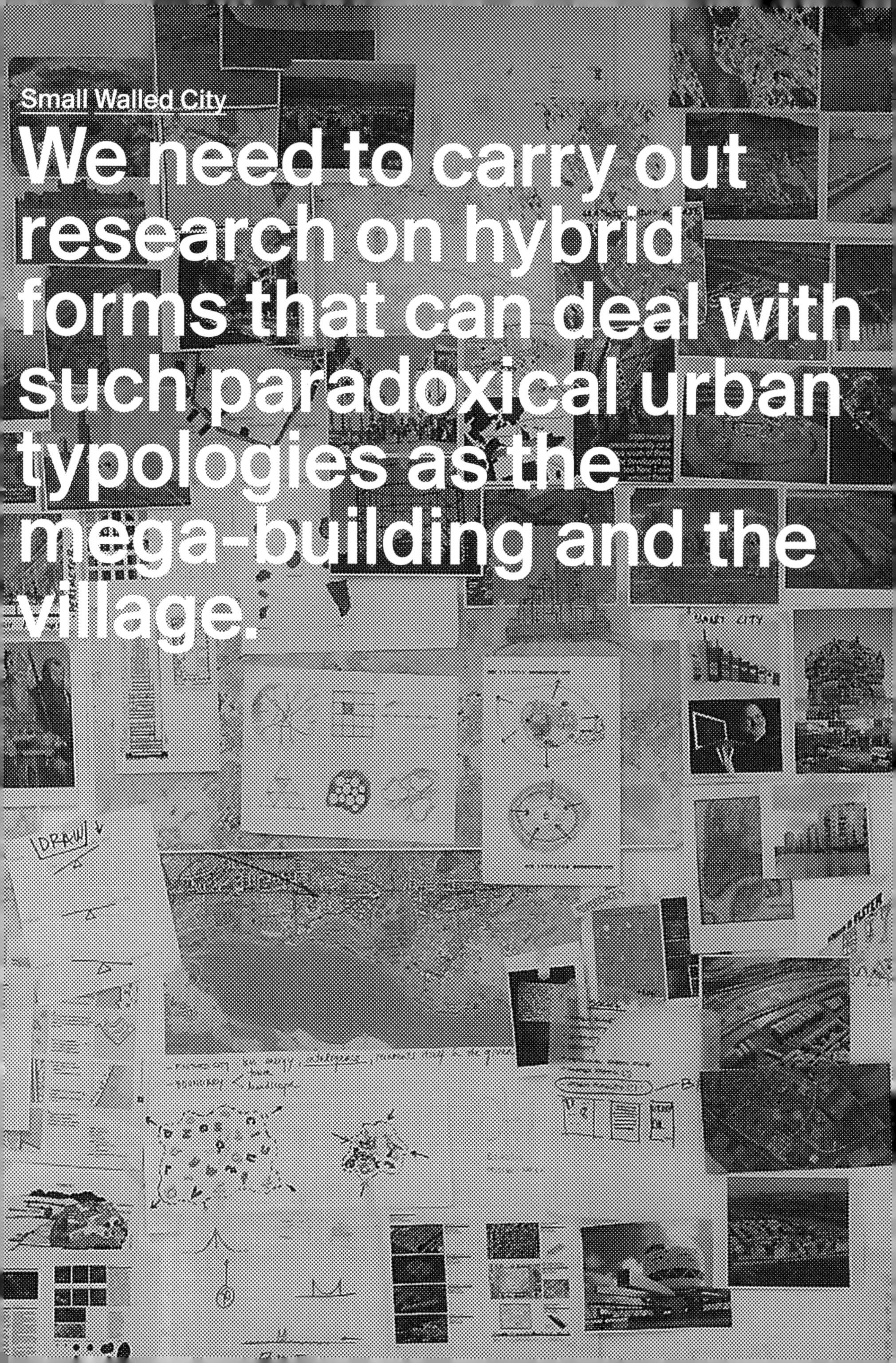

City and Landscape

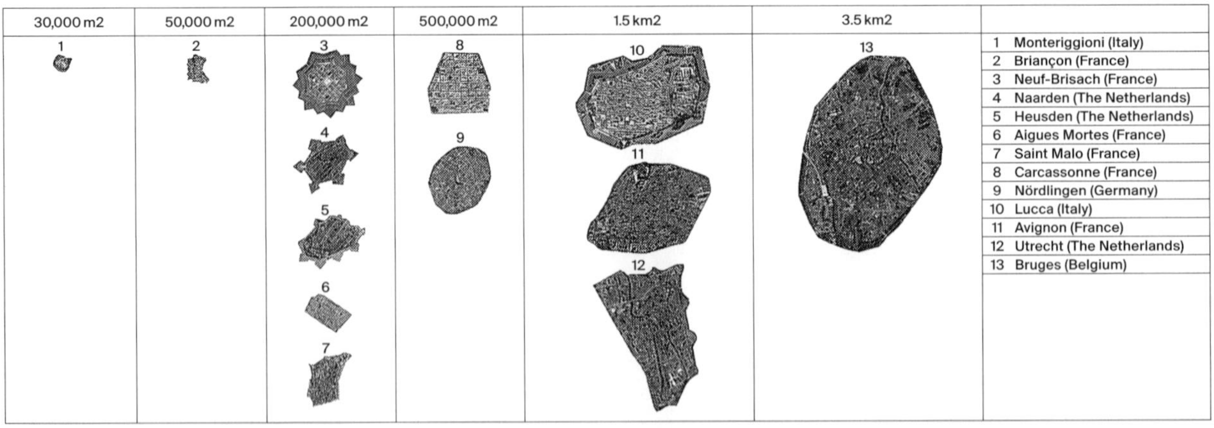

Carcassonne, France, built in the 6th Century BC

Aigues Mortes, France, built in 1248

Collage of walled cities in Glatttal

Defining Limit and Long-Term Densification

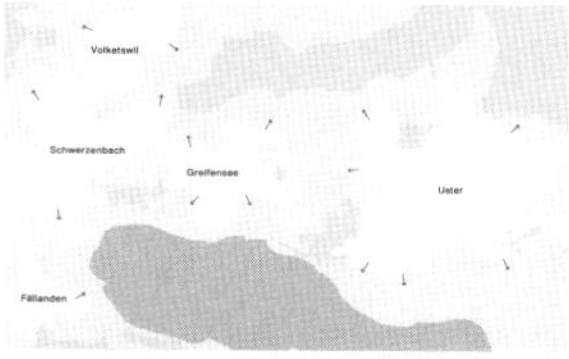

Expanding the settlement area

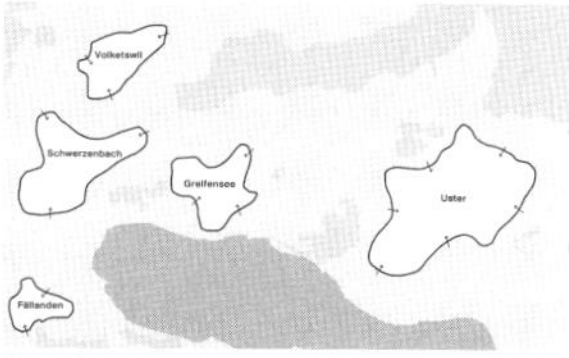

Creating edges

Uster with its new limit

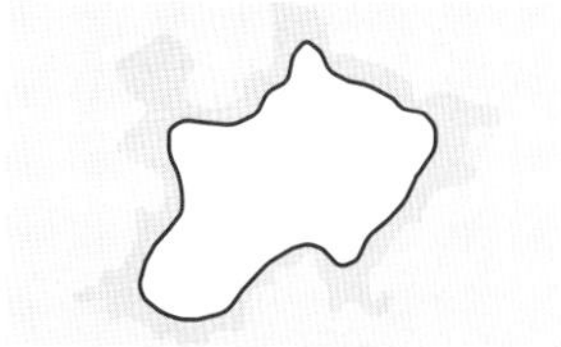
City interacting with landscape

Gradual densification of Uster: 2015

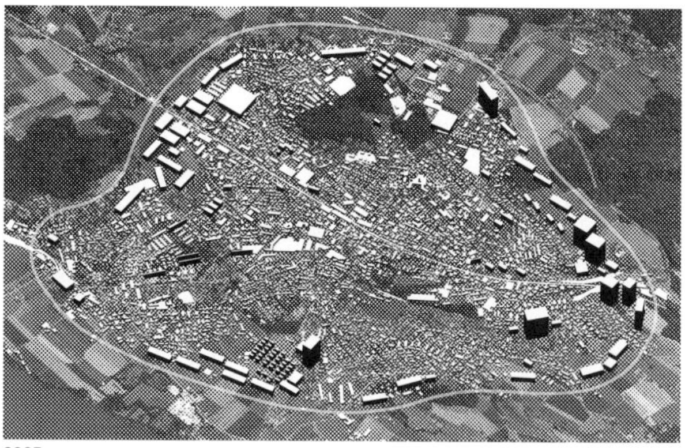
2025

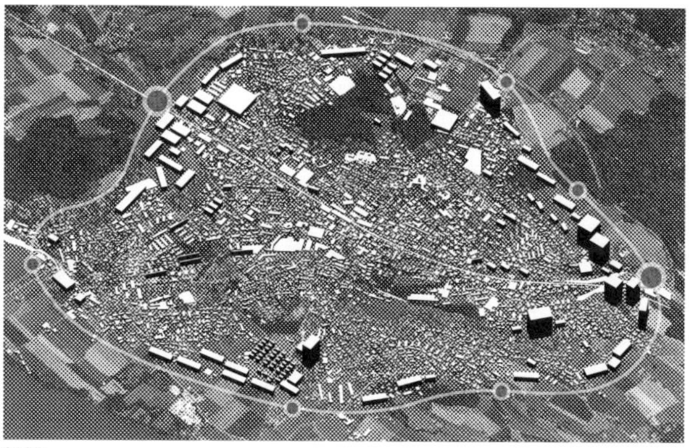
2035

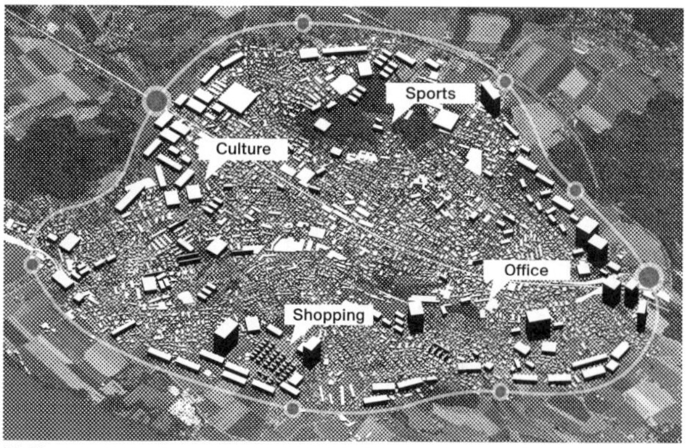

2045

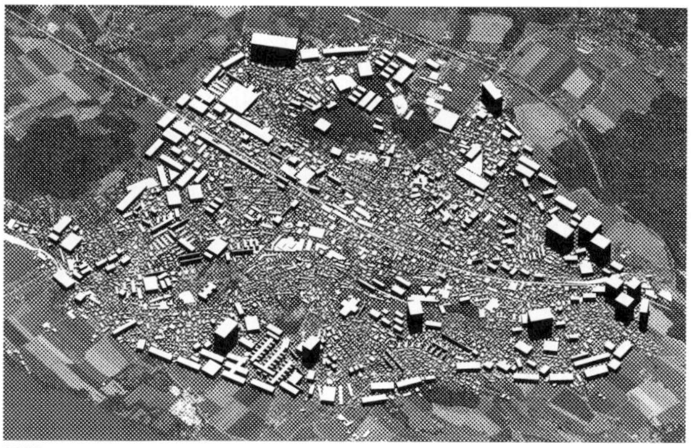
2055

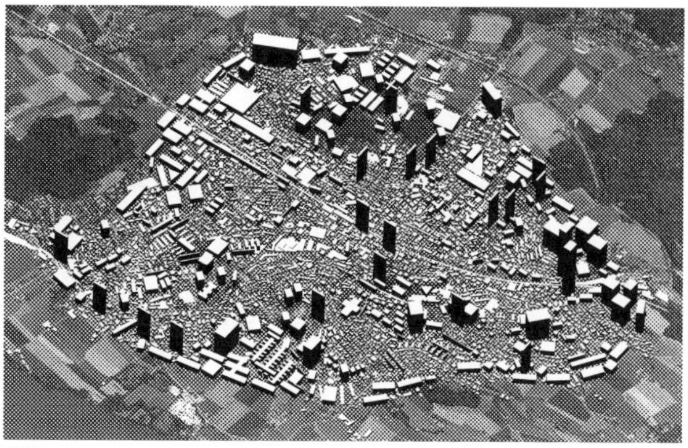
2065

SUITES & HOTEL

Studio G
Lecturer Mark Lee
Assistant Sharon Johnston-Lee
Students Andrea Alberto Dutto, Maria Letizia Garzoli, Larissa Geilen, Sara Jardim, Ariana Valentina Méndez Jimenez, Tobias Reinhardt, Jure Sadar, Wolke Vandenberghe, Meruert Zharekesheva

Placing the focus on investigating island and archipelago organizations as an alternative urban form for the landscape park area of the Glatttal, the studio applied the density provided by Krokodil's Glatt—the City plan and redistributed the built fabric among four isolated islands of high density, approximately 500 meters in diameter.

Each island is assigned one of four arbitrary shapes: a triangle, a square, a pentagon, or a circle, creating an archipelago composed of a three-sided shape, a four-sided shape, a five-sided shape, and an all-sided shape. Furthermore, each island is assigned a particular program along with housing that serves the larger Glatttal region. The triangular island has the cultural center, the square island houses the shopping center, the pentagonal island the business center, and the circular island the civic center. The shapes, regardless of the associated ideologies—whether utopian or dystopian—provide each island with an immediate identity. Similar to the nine-square-grid exercise, the respective shapes broach the issues of edge, center, field, and figure, all at the same time. The programmatic theme of each island takes Glatttal's functionalism as a city to an extreme.

Subsequently, the triangular island transformed Aldo Rossi's San Cataldo cemetery into a mega-structure by situating the entire development in the lake. The horizontal top surface of the building sits at the same level as the surface of the water, with the housing organized around the sunken courtyards.

In the pentagonal island, emphasis was placed on the establishment of hard boundaries as a means of distinguishing the interior from the exterior of the island. As a result, the island assumes an appearance that straddles between medieval and modern, with defined fortifications and small office towers emerging from within the walls.

The archipelago of four dense islands freed Glatttal's remaining open space and prevented further development, establishing an alphabet of urban morphology that is of its time and of all time.

Island Subcities

Characterized as dense developments demarcated by hard boundaries and surrounded by vast un-programmed areas, “Island Subcities” are concentrated attractors that could generate new urban fabric.

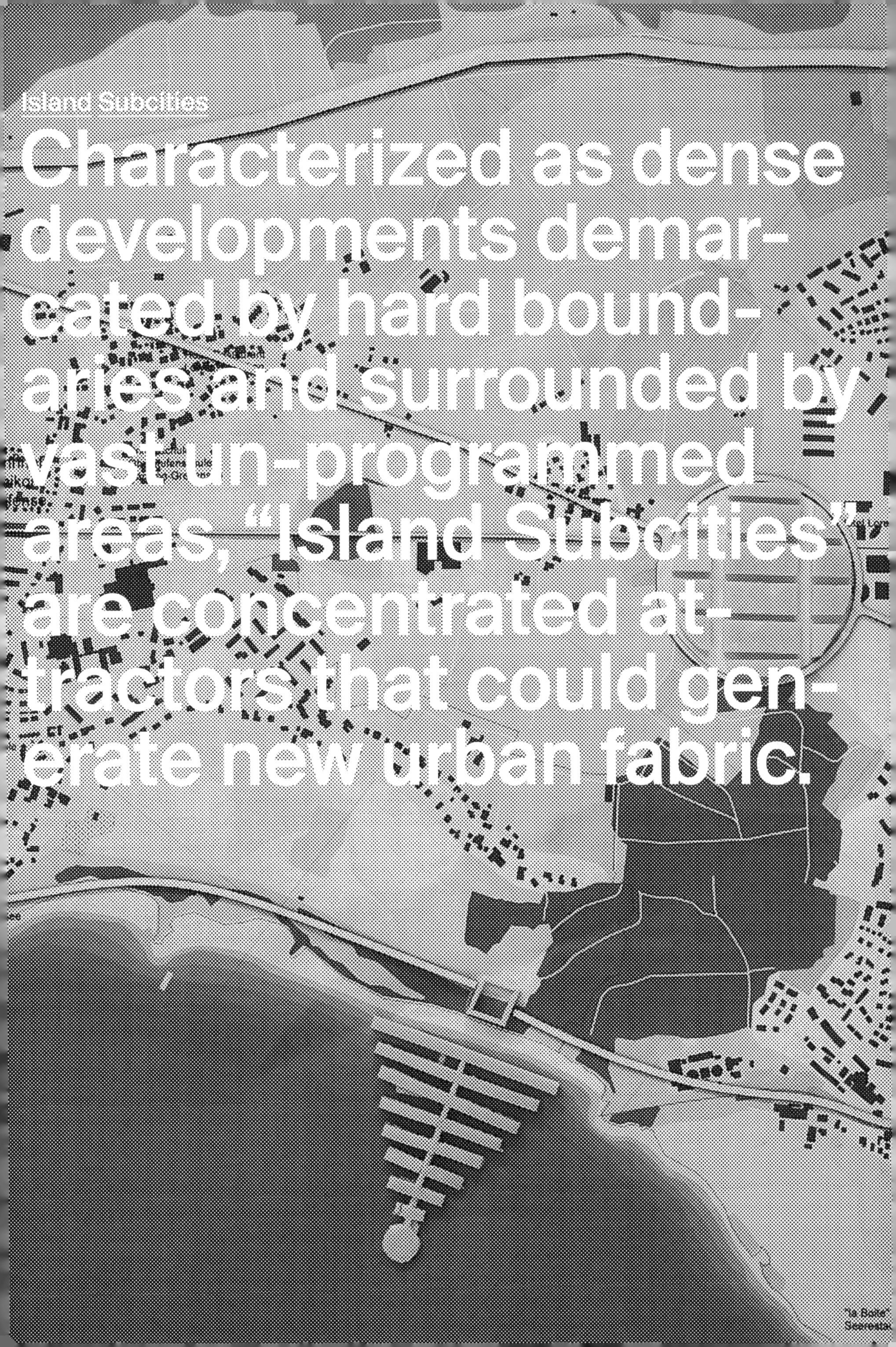

City grid studies

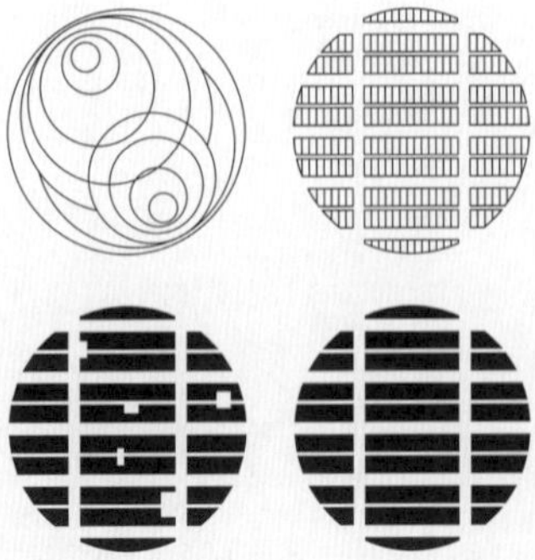

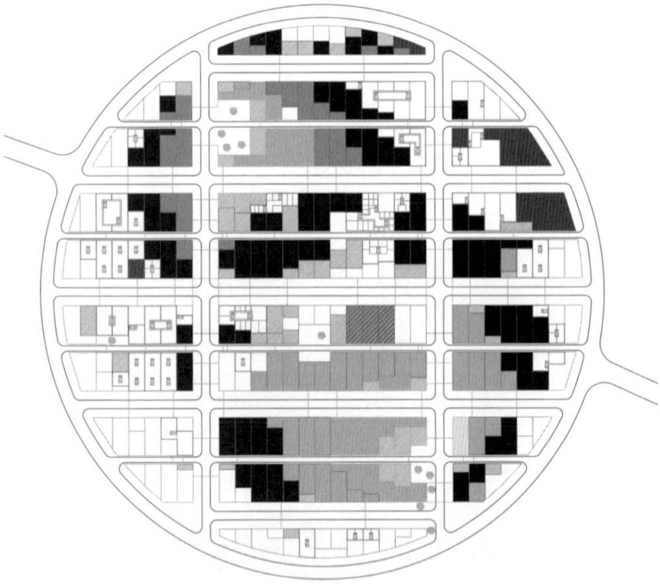

Ground floor

Circular Island

The circular island grafted an almost generic city grid plan as a point of departure, with an ambivalent resolution to the edges. In terms of section, the densification addresses the shape of the island by focusing around the perimeter. The island aspect is further reinforced by burying the thoroughfare in the cuts across the site.

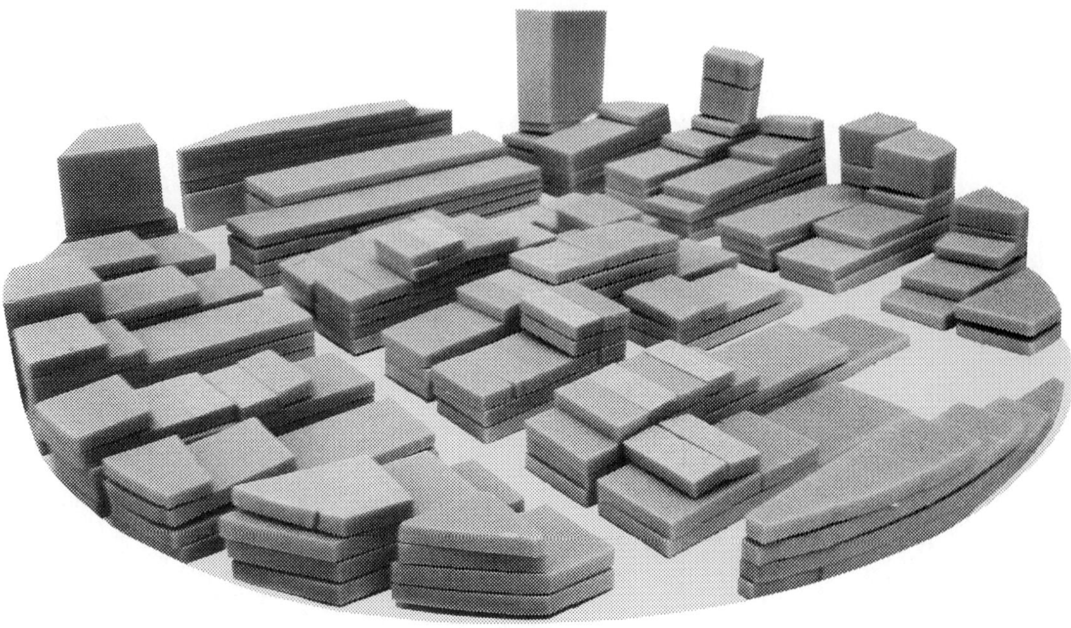

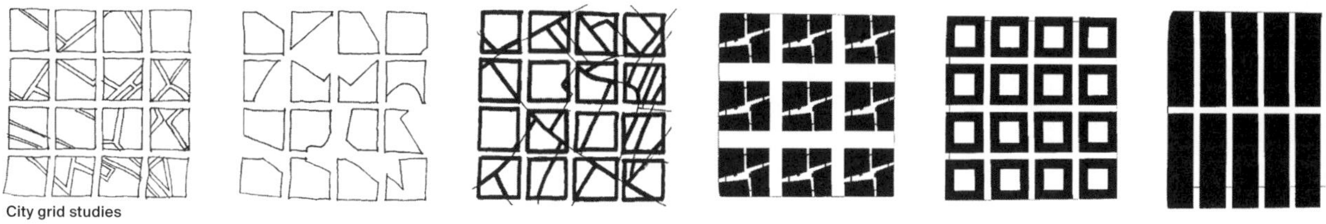
City grid studies

Ground floor

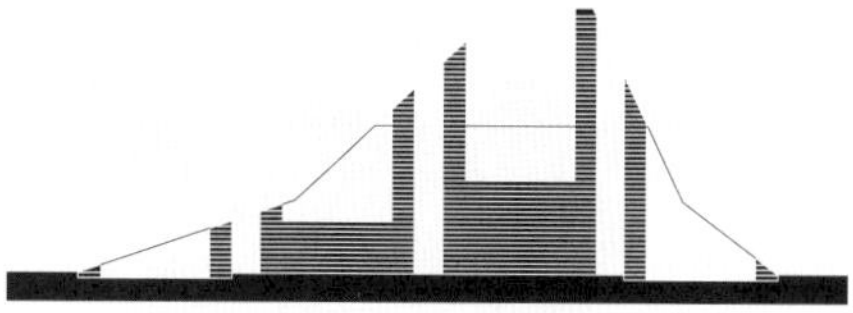

Square Island

The square island utilized the familiar perimeter block type while approximating the morphology of an artificial mountain, providing a special monumentality for the otherwise open landscape surrounding it. The internally-oriented shopping center is divided into sections so as to provide the vertical thrust of the mountain-like housing above it.

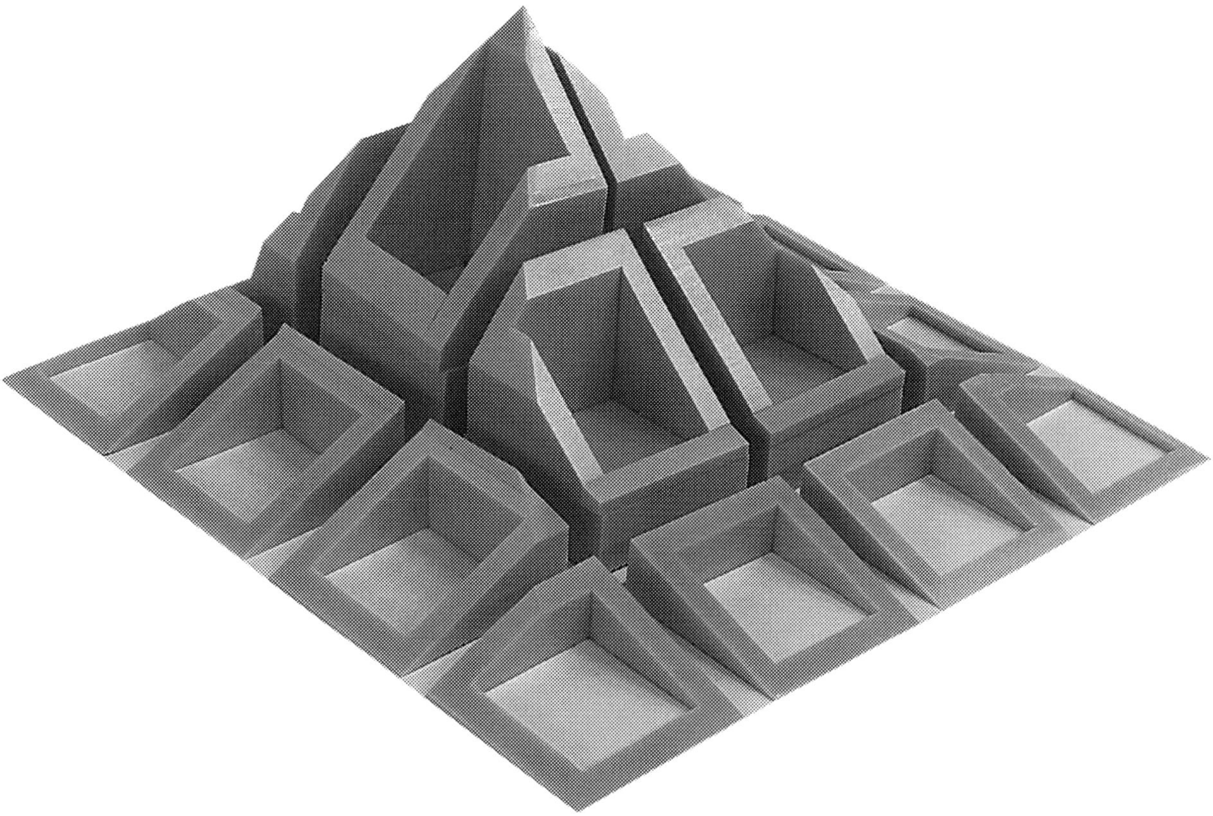

Résumé International Summer Academy Zurich

Markus Schaefer

Thanks a lot for the invitation Daniel and Mathias. It is an honor to be here and it has been a really fantastic day of reviews. I will try to summarize my impressions, which will be hard with all the input we received in just one day, but with a bit of support, I think I can do it. Unlike the studio presenters before me, I have no movie, no music, and no background activities, so I need your help. I propose that whenever you think I make a good point, when I get something right, you give me an ay, and when you disagree, you give me a nay, a bit like in the English parliament.

You are here at arguably one of the best architecture schools on the planet. I hope I can say this without any bias as I did not study here myself. However, urbanism and urban research still have a difficult position at this institution. I believe there are four different reasons for this: First, the generation of architects before us has with great skill and determination established the architectural object as the paradigmatic Swiss project, and this is what most students come here to study. ay!

Second, the Swiss building economy is still experiencing a boom that does not seem to be slowing down yet. Working on buildings is more lucrative than producing urban plans, and thanks to the open competition system, the market is also accessible to young architects. There is very little need for a niche strategy in today's economic climate. Third, **Switzerland does not have a very strong urban design culture and has few instruments to design the large scale.** Regional *planning* on the other hand is well established. As a result, Zurich, like many other regions, is shaped mainly by infrastructure, not by design. Lastly, and this is critical, from my outsider's point of view, **there is a lack of a clear academic basis, a theoretical foundation for urbanism that is both coherent and innovative.** Studios are either interested in new ideas and lack foundation—so there is not quite enough *Think* in the *Tank* clapping nay! ay! —or they are steeped in erudition but lack trust in the new. Compared to the precision with which architecture studios are taught, urban design lacks clarity and is often treated, by students and professors alike, as an afterthought, a discipline struggling for recognition. Even professionals outside academia bemoan the fact that precisely in an era of urban growth we have few instruments and very little theory to work with. I assume that this is about to change

through a series of initiatives, new appointments, and platforms like the ONA building we are currently in, but in today's situation, producing such a master plan for a city in the Glatttal as well as organizing the summer course you participated in is a much bigger achievement than you visitors can probably imagine. The organizers of this course therefore deserve a lot of credit. ay! clapping

In this summer course you worked in the very specific context of Switzerland. **Ours is a nation which for years and even centuries stubbornly resisted the accumulation of power and the development of an urban center.** We are as proud of our process of decision-making as of the distribution both of political power and urban mass. This tradition stems from the peculiar make-up of the country where a lot of responsibility is vested in the municipality leading to a distributed and often fragmented decision-making process. And in few countries in the world do politicians on the provincial and national levels have so much responsibility yet so little actual power. Only recently has an understanding of the metropolitan scale of Zurich been emerging. Zurich is increasingly understood as a polycentric urban region, a functional region, which is much larger than the core city. Only as the sum of its parts is it able to compete on a global scale. We need a better understanding of the metropolitan region as well as a political process and planning instruments to ensure that the region withstands current development pressures and retains its qualities.

Now *you* of course, or at least many of you, come from very different backgrounds. **Cities all over the globe are changing rapidly, and in our current multi-polar world system they develop in many different directions. Some cities transform in a well-planned manner, some grow informally. Some cities grow, others shrink. Cities sprawl, functional regions emerge, and new contenders appear.** According to McKinsey, the middle-weight cities will be the largest source by far of overall global economic growth. And each individual city by no means develops homogeneously. In a process of *urban splintering*, cities fragment into areas well connected to the global economy and areas left behind. We also observe a decoupling of cities from nations. London as a city, for example, is a successful, globalized urban center. England, as a nation, on the other hand, is a struggling State suffering from an ailing infrastructure, lack of an industrial base, and demographic as well as social shifts. The contemporary city system is truly global and interconnected in many ways. A global periphery no longer exists. Almost every place on earth is part of the contemporary urban system in one way or another. There is no place we can go and start anew.

As a result of this development, we can observe a high degree of volatility and instability. We experience a lot of change, but have only a limited understanding of how this change comes about and how it could be controlled. We have no clear answers or directives.

We are still working on cities very much like alchemists with many preconceived notions, some dogmata, the occasional brilliant insight, but very few hard facts. We are a frustratingly fragmented discipline. At the same time, we are faced with two new developments that question our methods: On the one hand, large corporations are discovering cities as the next big thing. Siemens started a new division focusing on cities and infrastructure. IBM, Cisco, McKinsey, and many other multinationals are entering the area of urban development because the scale and complexity of cities legitimize their business models and global perspectives. Eco-cities or *smart-cities* are being developed like products. We will be forced to deal with these complex and complicated technological cities in the future. It would be very good to have alternatives to them. The other extreme is the informal city, the phenomenon studied by Urban-Think Tank. Many of the most rapidly developing urban centers are characterized by a lack of control. In order to work on such cities, we will need to employ informal processes and new, technologically driven, bottom-up processes, which we have yet to understand. As a discipline, we are confronted with this spectrum of phenomena. Solutions—each with their own complexities—range from the total control seemingly required to achieve sustainability to the informal processes observed in reality.

Now what are cities exactly? Can we not come to a basic understanding of cities that informs and directs our work? **Cities are a technology for civilization invented eight to ten thousand years ago. They enable people to live close together and accumulate resources from a hinterland, which early on comprised the entire known world at the time.** Based on this resource surplus, social differentiation is possible. We call this variously culture, society, or public life. Cities enable interactions and protect transactions, constituting markets and economies. **Cities are about exchange and access, and access is defined not only by space but also by time.**

Time in turn is governed by infrastructure, and our infrastructures today are so incredibly powerful that they lead to large, sprawling cities, which are difficult to control. The suburbs you have been studying are ultimately the result of technological progress reshaping an ancient model. Cities act as catalysts, bringing people in contact to interact, transact, and live complex and differentiated lives.

Now, if we look at the studios as a series of case studies, we can see quite well the range of concepts and tools that architects and urban designers currently have at their disposal to deal with this complex situation. And again, I believe that these tools are not adequate yet, but let us analyze them quickly.

Some of these tools as well as the concerns they address are foreign to us Swiss practitioners because we live and work in very specific conditions, making your contributions all the more valuable.

Globalization makes us question hierarchies. *You* are teaching us as much as we can teach you, because there is no silver bullet for the current challenges we are facing.

If we compare the studios, we see different degrees of clarity regarding how the disciplines of architecture and urban design assert themselves in respect to other fields. I will now discuss the studios proceeding from the autonomous to the, let's say, *trans-disciplinary*. Autonomous architecture, originally referring to the work of Aldo Rossi, posits that architectural forms have intrinsic value and historic permanence while functions and social concerns change. By studying the material manifestation of architecture and its urban context—typology, iconography, and their history—new architecture can be inferred. Unfortunately, autonomy is often misunderstood to mean having a very clear idea of what the architectural object is while not being so interested in what this object does to its context. The architect as author, so the belief goes, is responsible to his own discipline only and his will to form in an act of utopian defiance against the vicissitudes of reality. Transdisciplinarity is the other end of the spectrum. It rests on the belief that only in the exchange between disciplines can architecture be relevant, culminating at its most extreme in a deep mistrust of the discipline and its responsibilities.

This brings us to Mark Lee's Studio, which I would describe as a kind of *Autonomous Urbanism*. The studio attempts to define urban form with the tools of the architect. **Form is seen as an act of resistance, an act against the entropy of suburbia.** But what kind of political power would someone need to produce a project on this scale, and what financial means would be required to take risks of this magnitude? Inherent in autonomous form, therefore, is a political message. It is a thought experiment in absolutist control, but all too easily this approach remains a utopian statement. And in today's permissive discourse, utopia more often than not is a safe haven, an academic game, which under the guise of *provocation* skirts real responsibility. That would be my assessment of this first studio. That would be my assessment of this first studio. You can give me an ay or a nay of course. laughter ay!

We have a second autonomous proposal in my opinion with David Trottin's "périphérique—drawing the line." **This proposal claims that an act of planning can be strong enough to contain this sprawling beast called suburbia.** The proposal consists of a line of infrastructure encircling and containing a settlement area. It advocates clear functional planning, ultimately a very modernist idea. It is inspired by the Transit Oriented Development movement that originated in the United States. But if cities are about access and if access is always resulting in gradients from the very accessible to the least accessible, then hard lines are not likely to occur, especially when the demarcation is infrastructure. The concept of a hard line in urban design is a desirable but difficult concept, hard to do and defensible only under very specific circumstances, as in the case of a city wall for example in the Middle Ages or as an internal void, such as New York's Central Park. Ay or nay? ay!

The third studio was taught by Martin Rein-Cano from Topotek and takes landscape as its starting point, a landscape "project" to be precise. There is a visible belief in the "project," a precise professional engagement with a found condition, both as a statement and as a tool for communication. Two points are noteworthy: first, the seductive appeal of form. The project is well done, worked out and detailed. It garners sympathies and with its precision allows for a concrete discussion. It cannot be trifled with. Second, **landscape is very much about defining relationships.** In cities that are not densely packed, landscape is a useful organizational element. If we occupy an open space with an architectural volume, it is difficult to make relations work, **but if we design a really well-considered open space as a kind of scaffold from which a stretch of peripheral city can draw identity, we have a surprising amount of power.** ay! clapping **So landscape is a powerful tool for organizing territory.** Even though the park is a formal statement that is quite alien to its context, it is more than a nicely shaped buffer space. It becomes a core element for the urban condition of the airport to transform into something new, for this infrastructural moment to be activated as an urban potential.
whoo! clapping

So these are three varieties of autonomy. The landscape is currently the frontrunner. It's a bit like the Olympic Games. We have a hypothetical winner. laughter

We have two studios that worked with the large scale. Boštjan Vuga's studio proposes to turn infrastructure into architecture. This idea also originated in modernity and was rediscovered in the 1990s in various academic settings. **Since infrastructure is so effective in shaping a territory, is it possible to join forces, co-opt it, and take advantage of it? Can we not architecturalize it and turn it into something urban?** Since "form follows infrastructure" in many different ways, this is not a bad idea. But in this project, the devil is in the details. The highway would need to be changed in many ways to allow for multiple access points. As a result, transit traffic would suffer. The proposed train line would be expensive and lack passengers. The infrastructural axis would need to be bridged in many more locations for the two sides to grow together. But do these areas have enough urban potential to warrant such an investment? For this infrastructural strategy to work, a detailed understanding and development of accessibility is critical, accompanied by a precise understanding of development mechanisms, finances, and political processes between the different stakeholders.

The next studio also proposes a landscape scheme that proves again to be quite successful. Christophe Girot and Lukas Schweingruber employ landscape as an armature of identity that orchestrates and structures peripheral growth. Landscape is an interesting tool because it

provides identity and legitimacy. It seems to represent the non-human, the non-semantic, and the absolute. It is hard to contest a landscape concept as it is not immediately read as a cultural object. It organizes a form of urbanity, with financial means only available in an urban context, yet it is not understood as urban. So one more point for the landscape architects. ay! clapping **The project takes ideas from the network city concept ("Netzstadt") that has been developed at the ETH. It is concerned with orchestrating metabolic flows in the context of an ecological urbanism. Identity and ecological quality of a landscape can really add value to the mosaic of locations, which in the end makes the metropolitan region of Zurich work, like any urban region.** An urban region should allow for as many options, as much potential, as many choices and niches, on as small and accessible a terrain as possible.

Another person working on the large scale is Don Murphy from VMX with the project *coastline management* as I would call it. He started his studio with a series of *blind dates* to illustrate the many random interactions that constitute urbanity. In the process, he managed to charm his students into absolute submission and make them state that we should not hate suburbia. The studio argues that Switzerland is about suburbia, is about idyllic life in a green landscape. We have the good fortune to live this idyllic life so close to an urban center. With large scale measures that increase the quality of this green area and at the same time direct growth, the studio proposes to manage sprawl almost like a natural phenomenon. **It is attractive to think that in the end, the metropolitan region of Zurich, in fact, Switzerland as a whole, might be nothing more than a well-made Los Angeles.** Is this an ay? ay! clapping

The last of the large scale studios was taught by Anne-Julchen Bernhardt and Jörg Leeser from BeL Associates. I am not sure what I should call their approach, maybe *reinventing pragmatism*? Their project is about accepting a pre-existing context, both the territory and the cultural mechanisms acting upon it. **They propose a forced marriage between the ideal of the public commons ("die Allmend") and the Oklahoma land rush, the belief that in the balance of power between collective ideals and a liberalized market something unexpectedly public could emerge.** Behind this proposal is the idea that simple rules can have complex results, that planning can emerge from bottom-up processes when the mechanisms are well designed. The large scale, therefore, is the sum of all individual decisions held in check by a few deeply held collective convictions—a surprisingly apt description of the status quo. We have now seen three autonomous studios, three large scale studios, and even though the project of this studio was not entirely clear to me, the general idea behind it is interesting. Ay or nay? ay!

We now reach the next contenders. I would call them *transfers*. Again, there are three of them. Kunlé Adeyemi proposes a version of "learning from" introduced into the discourse so famously by Venturi and Scott-Brown. The studio starts from urban research and studies three prototypical cities that are all uniquely defined by specific forms of access, by foot in Mumbai, by bus in Curitiba, and by telecom services in Lagos. Here once again, form follows infrastructure. The physical structure of these cities is a result of their regime of accessibility. Soft forms of access, such as telecom networks, are a key to understanding, and play a role in any urban design proposal. At the same time, they are hard to plan and difficult to control, but what is so inspiring about the cities the studio looked at is urbanity in its raw form. **These cities develop without much control and hence offer the possibility of looking at urbanity as something almost ecological. Urbanity is visibly emergent, iconoclastic, and vital.** Compared to this, our understanding of European cities seems overly static, too proper, and fatally binary in our clear differentiation of private and public, of perimeter block and open space. **European cities work well when they are dense, but they reach limits when the space requirement is multiplied by the aspirations and needs of today's individuals, such as the 54 m2 of average gross living area of an individual in Zurich. The city becomes bloated and exhibits all the problems that we see here in Zurich-Oerlikon.** Kunlé's concerns are an important antidote to that. ay! It's an ay. Fantastic!

Then we have Urban-Think Tank, Hubert Klumpner and Alfredo Brillembourg who propose a process of negotiation. They take inspiration from cities that grow, from cities that change, which have that kind of fertility. They take Kunlé's preoccupation to the next level. However, in cities that are shaped by such bottom-up processes, power takes the role of the legal framework and rules that are imposed top-down. Depending on the culture, this means brute force, money, or access to authorities. In the case of planners, it means power of persuasion. I think the two tutors exemplify this very clearly when they, like two community workers or process master planners, by sheer force of personality, energy, and persuasion, move their studio in a particular direction. I think this approach has great potential and will be indispensable in the growing cities of the future. But Switzerland resists the accumulation of power. Decisions are taken by consensus and governed by rules and regulations. I do not mind consensus if it guarantees me a good quality of life.

Yet, are we flexible enough in Switzerland to keep up with rapid developments in the world? Will we be competitive in an urban future? This is an interesting discussion to have. A key insight from this studio is that globalization does not generate sameness everywhere. When we transfer methods and insights from one context to another, we need to understand both the original as well as the new context in order for the transfer to be meaningful. This is an insight that EM2N contributed to our symposium *Learning from Tokyo* earlier this year in Zurich. I think this is an ay too. ay!

Now, the last studio taught by Arno Brandlhuber, Christopher Roth, and Sam Chermayeff, proposes a *discourse*. We reached the very end of our spectrum from the very clear disciplinary and autonomous, via the large scale and planning, to the newer approaches, the non-project-oriented approaches. **This studio represents the most extreme case. It focuses entirely on discourse. Behind this position is the understanding that when architects work, they always define. Any line an architect puts on paper excludes other possibilities.** By remaining on the level of discourse, the studio proposes to keep possibilities open longer, avoid jumping to conclusions, and delaying the rigidity of a project. The approach offers to charge a project with meaning in an almost poetic and purely semantic way and at the same time, keep all possibilities open. But how can we achieve this? Already the Structuralists told us that the definition of opposites is always a first response in semantics, that opposite terms are to semantics what platonic forms are to geometry. Whenever we do not engage with context or do not have a very clear idea where we want to go, generating opposites is always a good first step because you generate meaning without having to understand the situation too precisely. The danger is that the discourse becomes purely self-referential.

And with that, the circle closes and we reach again the autonomous architects and planners in the very beginning, so we have a circle where we went from autonomy to the large scale to different urban research studios again to a discursive autonomy. This shows how limited our tool set still is, how easily we get caught up in self-referential discussion, and how hard it is to deal with reality.

So what is the conclusion? What are the lessons we have learned? How can we teach the crocodile to plan? laughter The group envisions a master plan for a city of 400,000 inhabitants. In the Swiss context, this project is important. It is a political provocation, it is an illustration of a potential and it is agitation. I think this is quite interesting even though **I am doubtful and critical about the use of the tool master plan to convey this kind of concept. Nevertheless, they produced a project that is readable, understandable, and clear.** I hope that this infusion of global intelligence that you provide enables the crocodile to evolve in a more mammalian direction. laughter clapping

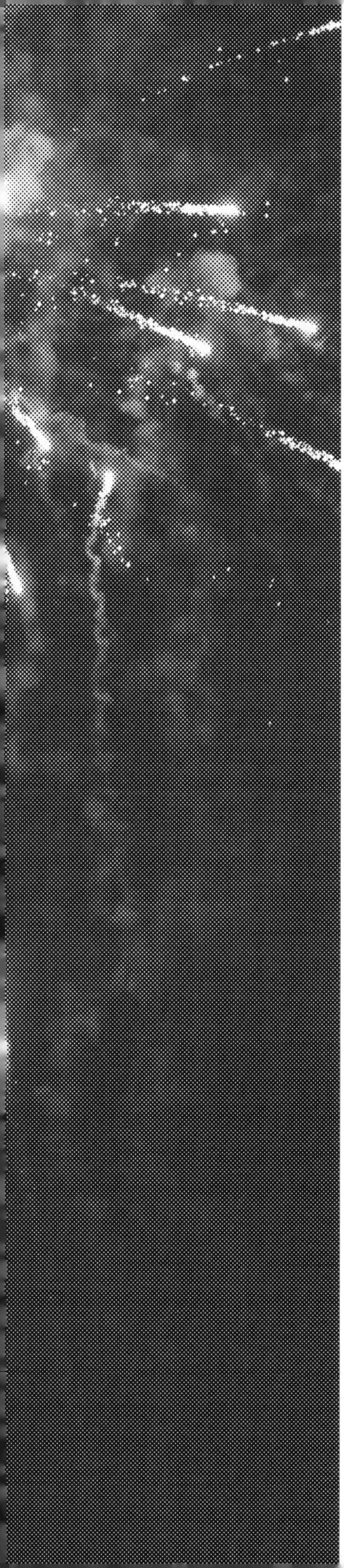

And what can *we* take from it? As I said at the beginning, we will face enormous challenges with cities in a future of volatile development. On the one hand, cities are the source of many of the problems we are facing in terms of resource depletion, a shortage of space, and demographic changes. On the other hand, our global urban system is the only solution to house and feed so many people on this increasingly small planet. So cities will be the main problem in the near future.

I already explained that many people are interested in this business of cities. It should be our generation's goal to ensure that we do this as intelligently and honestly as we possibly can, since the future we are facing will not be easy. **We need cities that are resilient, cities that can thrive also when parameters change, because they will. For this we need an almost ecological understanding of cities that is supported by a phenomenology of the specific and a science of the generic.** We need to end the era of alchemy, we need to come out of our postmodern niches, put our historicizing dogmata behind us, and leave academia's ivory towers. We need to rediscover the project *city* in all its many aspects and we need to do it now. And I believe that the work of the Architects Group Krokodil and this Summer Academy is truly a great contribution in this direction. Thanks a lot.

clapping shouting

Text based on résumé delivered on August 4, 2012
at the International Summer Academy Zurich

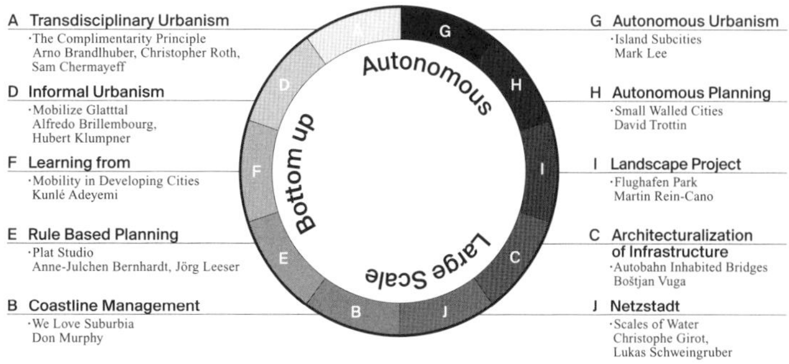

Encyclopedia

A

Absence **1.** ˈæbsəns, from the Latin *absentia*, describes the lack or the non-existence of something. **2.** Once an object, a moment, a condition is described, its opposite also exists, namely its ‘non-existence’. If something is made into a theme then its possible lack is, of necessity, also included—at least implicitly. However, the inductive argument *a contrario* does not allow us to assume that a lack indicates the possible existence of something. **3.** *Absence:* The most beautiful is not to be present. *(Rem Koolhaas, S,M,L,XL)* ↗ ⊠, ↗ 1m2/sec 08/15, ↗ Studio A

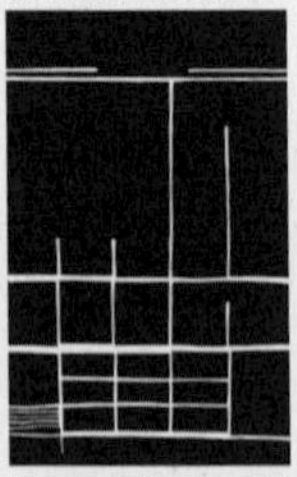
Newspaper without contents

Abstraction **1.** æbˈstrækʃn̩, from the Latin *abstractus* ‘removed’, perfect participle passive of *abstrahere* ‘to remove’, ‘separate’. **2.** In its European phase, abstract art developed in a context of theoretical and social concerns involved in the task of creating an ideal society. These roles were often articulated in manifestos associated with various movements, such as Constructivism, Suprematism, and the Bauhaus. The tendency in abstraction to use geometric form and to achieve compositional unity through the reduction of naturalistic forms brings to mind Hegel’s thesis that progress is a process of dematerialization, the triumph of spirit (rationality) over matter. In this context, aesthetic value is found primarily in the role of artworks as precocious exemplars of the future, and only secondarily in their purely aesthetic qualities. *(ea)* ↗ 1m2/sec 08/15, ↗ Incremental Masterplanning

Adeyemi, Kunlé Kunlé Adeyemi, who was born in 1976, is an architect, designer, and urbanist with a track record of conceiving and completing high profile, high quality projects internationally. Born and raised in Nigeria, Adeyemi studied architecture at the University of Lagos where he began his early practice, before joining *OMA* in 2002. He later studied at Princeton University and received a post-professional master’s degree in architecture. His office *NLÉ* (‘at home’ in Yoruba) is an architecture, design, and urbanism practice committed to the business and intelligence of developing cities. ↗ ⊠, ↗ Studio F, ↗ Lecturer

Kunlé Adeyemi

Agglomeration by Peter Fischli & David Weiss

Agglomeration **1.** əˌglɒməˈreɪʃn̩, from the medieval Latin *agglomeratio* ‘conglomeration’, ‘concentration’, (Swiss) conurbation. *(d1)* **2.** In Switzerland the definition is made up of two parts: *a)* agglomerations are contiguous areas made up of several municipalities with a total of at least 20,000 inhabitants. *b)* every agglomeration has a central zone consisting of the core municipality and, possibly, further municipalities, each with at least 2,000 workplaces and at least 85 workplaces per 100 resident employed persons. In addition, these municipalities must send at least 1/6 of their employed persons to work in the core municipality, be connected with it in terms of buildings, or border on it. *(r)* ↗ Preface, ↗ 1m2/sec 08/15, ↗ Studio E, I, ↗ *Glatttal*, ↗ *Long-Term Photographic Observation …*, ↗ *Zwischenstadt* **3.** The interest in anti-beauty, the view of the familiar, an openness towards an effect that shows how very ordinary, unspectacular, and dry things can newly stimulate our perception. This is what Peter Fischli and David Weiss awaken with their series of photographs *Siedlungen, Agglomeration* (1993). They look at the most real of all our worlds between city and country, look into the atmosphere of Swiss suburbs that permeates everything yet is hard to define. They do this with a camera held at eye level that underlines the undramatic, observing attitude. In contemporary art this approach is called ‘as found’ and is connected with Duchamp, among others. ↗ ⊠, ↗ *Duchamp, Marcel*, ↗ *Found Poem*

Analysis **1.** əˈnæləsəs, from the Greek *análysis* ‘dissolution’, ‘dismemberment’. **2.** Defined as the process of breaking a concept down into simpler parts, or into its components, so that its logical structure is displayed. Before the process of decomposition can take place, the issues to be analyzed must first be translated into a subjectively ‘correct’ logical form, suggesting that analysis also involves a transformative or interpretive dimension. It is one of the first steps in the process of ‘planning’. *(o)* **3.** Creative urban planning is revealed as a dialectic process, if it is understood less in the sense of a strict chronological sequence—first problem finding (analysis) then problem solving, and more as an analytical relationship that oscillates between rethinking and reframing. *(Angelus Eisinger)* ↗ Mission Statement, ↗ Incremental Masterplanning, ↗ Studio A, ↗ *Planning*

Angélil, Marc Marc Angélil, who was born in 1954 in Egypt, is an architect and professor at the Department of Architecture at the ETH Zurich. His research at the Network City and Landscape (NSL) and the Future Cities Laboratory (FCL) in Singapore addresses the development of large metropolitan regions. He is the author of several books on urban transformation in developing countries. He runs his architectural practice *agps* with Sarah Graham, Manuel Scholl, Reto Pfenninger, and Hanspeter Oester, with offices in Los Angeles and Zurich. ↗ ⊠, ↗ 1m2/sec 08/15, ↗ *Lecturer*

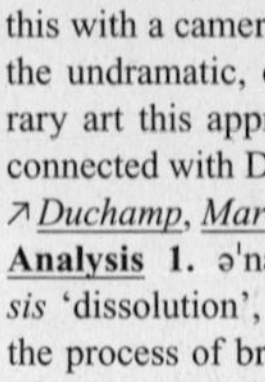
Marc Angélil

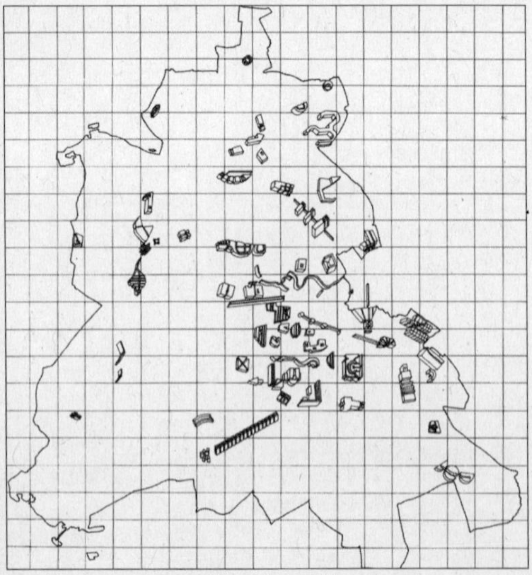
Berlin as an archipelago, by Oswald Mathias Ungers

Archipelago **1.** ˌɑːkɪˈpeləgəʊ, from the Greek *arkhi-* ‘chief’ and *pélagos* ‘sea’, also ‘dominated waters’, ‘maritime region rich in islands’. An archipelago is a synonym for a group of islands, a collection of islands relatively close to each other. **2.** In this context, ‘archipelago’ is a metaphorical term for the concept of *the city in the city* and represents an urban planning principle of Oswald Mathias Ungers, the condensing of individual zones (‘islands’) within a city while at the same time forming green open areas between them. Developed during a Summer Academy in 1977, the *Green City Archipelago* was discussed as a possible future concept for the thinned out, de-industrialised city of Berlin. ↗ ⊠, ↗ Identity Markers …, ↗ Book chapter Archipelago, ↗ Studio C, H, G, ↗ *Ungers, O. M.*, ↗ *Island Subcities*

Architects Group Krokodil The Architects Group Krokodil, founded in 2009 and managed by *Boltshauser*, *EM2N*, *pool*, *Schweingruber Zulauf*, and *Zierau*, postulates a change of paradigms for Swiss planning culture and substantiates this using the example of Glatttal in the Zurich metropolitan area. Based on the assumption that a city has to be wanted and that it has to be designed, Krokodil claims that Glatttal should not be read as a peripheral metropolitan region made up of individual communities, but as an emerging urban body. This reading produces a proposal for even more inten-

Architects Group Krokodil

Association’s logo

sive access systems and a significant increase in density. The core message of the Glatttal city is a plea to preserve difference. City should remain city and country should remain country. ↗ ⊠ ⊠, ↗ Mission Statement

Attitude **1.** ˈætɪtjuːd, from the French *attitude*, and the Latin *aptitudo* 'usefulness', the internalised approach towards all imaginable social, psychological, cognitive, normative, and other phenomena that affect behavior and action by selecting and arranging. Attitudes are, on the one hand, the result of selection processes that the individual in the socialization process makes his own from the almost infinite variety of possible ways of thinking and behaving,while on the other they form the basis for being able to react and act in a relatively secure way. *(u)* ↗ *Typology Transfer*, ↗ Retrofitting Suburbia

Audience **1.** ˈɔːdiəns, from Latin *audientia*, from the present participle *audiens* 'hearing', from the verb *audio* 'I hear'; a person or group of (usually) people viewing a show (film, play, performance) or the readership of a publication. *(w)* **2.** Intellectuals need an audience, a circle of people to whom they can address themselves and who can bestow recognition. *(Rem Koolhaas, S,M,L,XL)* ↗ ⊠, ↗ Complementary to *Lecturer*

Audience at the Summer Academy

Autobahn Inhabited Bridges (AIB) **1.** ˈɔːtəʊbɑːn ɪnˈhæbɪtɪd ˈbrɪdʒɪz; Autobahn (motorway) bridge (noun): *a)* bridge that forms part of a highway, *b)* a bridge that crosses over a motorway; inhabited (adjective): having inhabitants, lived in. *(d1)* **2.** Autobahn Inhabited Bridges are big and slightly awkward structures that bridge over the highway and connect locations on either side. The AIB are hybrid buildings but have defined primary uses. They are large scale interventions; they are incomplete, capable of adapting to various changes occurring throughout seasons and years. They are permanent and temporary at the same time; they are a building and a park, an infrastructure and an interior. They are not only connectors, but are themselves also a destination. And, first and foremost, they are tools of identification. They are triggers of and for future urban transformation. ↗ Studio C, ↗ *Building Typologies*, ↗ *Hybrid Buildings*

Autonomous Urbanism **1.** ɔːˈtɒnəməs ˈɜːbəˌnɪzm, 'autonomous' (adjective): from the Greek *autos* 'self' and *nomos* 'law'; describes independence or self-rule as opposed to heteronomy. 'Urbanism' (noun): from the Latin *urbs* 'city' and *urbanus* 'belonging to the city'; characteristic of the city, of city life. **2.** Autonomous urbanism postulates an intrinsic value and historic consistency of architectural form, whereas the function changes. Autonomous architecture is the opposite of transdisciplinarity, although a graduated spectrum lies between these two concepts within which architecture and urban planning are understood more or less as one among several disciplines that work on the city. The term 'autonomous urbanism' also includes buildings that are arbitrarily positioned in the urban landscape. These buildings represent only themselves and, while they do not lead to the further development of the city in which they stand, at the same time they cannot, themselves, become city. **3.** This term is often associated with the work of Aldo Rossi. ↗ Studio C, G, H, ↗ Résumé …

B

Barbecue ˈbɑːbɪkju; used as a noun, the term can refer to the meat, the cooking apparatus itself (the 'barbecue grill' or simply 'barbecue'), or to the party that includes such food or such preparation methods. Grilled veal sausages are one of Zurich's specialities. *(w)* ↗ *Beer*, ↗ *Sausage*

Bassersdorf *Municipality type:* residential suburban community, *region:* Glatttal, *district:* Bülach, *post code:* 8303, *official municipality key:* 52, *population:* 11,157, *population density (residents/km2):* 1,241. *Height above sea level:* 460 m, *area (ha):* 899. *(st)* Bassersdorf probably has the biggest and most important Fasnacht (carnival celebration) in the Zürcher Unterland (Zurich lowlands). The name is pronounced ˈbasərzˌdɔrf, or in the local dialect ˈbɒsərʃˌtoːrfː or, abbreviated, Basi ˈbɑzi. ↗ *Glatt—the City*

Glattgold Beer

Beer bɪə, from Proto-Indo-European *bews-* 'dross', 'sediment', 'brewer's yeast'; every evening during the Summer Academy there were sausages and beer, for instance *Turbinenbräu*, *Glattgold* or a *Club Mate*. ↗ ⊠, ↗ *Barbecue*

BeL Associates ↗ *Bernhardt, Anne-Julchen*, ↗ *Leeser, Jörg*

Benoît, Jean-Jacques In the film *Glatt—The City* by the Architects Group Krokodil, Jean-Jacques Benoît, the young and dynamic correspondent from the western, French-speaking part of Switzerland, was sent to the city of Glatt as exchange-journalist to interview the residents of Glatt and to report on the new city from his 'foreign' viewpoint. ↗ ⊠, ↗ *Glatt—the City*

Jean-Jacques Benoît

Bernhardt, Anne-Julchen Anne-Julchen Bernhardt, who was born in 1971, worked as an architect in Berlin and Cologne and as assistant professor at the University of Aachen. Since 2008 she has been a tenured professor for building typologies at RWTH Aachen University. In 2000, she and Jörg Leeser established *BeL Associates*. They have received numerous awards. The office has worked on 95 projects, of which 15 have been completed. ↗ ⊠, ↗ Studio E, ↗ *BeL Associates*, ↗ *Lecturer*

Anne-Julchen Bernhardt

Bideau, André André Bideau, who was born in 1966, is an architectural theorist, lecturer, and writer in Zurich. He graduated with a degree in architecture from the ETH, and completed his doctorate at Zurich University. From 1997 to 2002 he was the editor of *Werk, Bauen + Wohnen*; and in 2004, Research Fellow at the Internationales Forschungszentrum Kulturwissenschaften (IFK) in Vienna. In addition to his work as architecture critic and lecturing posts in Europe and the U.S., Bideau is working on a research project that examines the connections between architectural discourses since 1968 and the experience of postmodern urbanity. ↗ ⊠, ↗ Identity Markers …, ↗ *Lecturer*

André Bideau

Black **1.** blæk, from the Old English blæc 'black', 'dark', from Proto-Germanic *blakaz*, *blakkaz* 'burnt'; originally derived from 'bleach', from Proto-Indo-European *bhleg-* 'to burn' or 'to shine', compare with Latin *flagare* 'to shine', *flagrare* 'to burn'. **2.** The color perceived in the absence of light. ↗ *Absence* **3.** In the lecture of Marc Angélil, black stands for infrastructure. ↗ 1m2/sec 08/15, ↗ *Green*, ↗ *Red*

Boltshauser, Roger Roger Boltshauser, who was born in 1964, studied architecture in Lucerne and at ETH Zurich. He founded his own practice in Zurich in 1996, whose projects are largely the outcome of competitions and study commissions and are characterized by powerful, block-like depositions with a high density in terms of space and materials. The office has also made a name for itself in rammed earth construction, as illustrated by the Rauch House in Schlins, Austria and the school pavilion *Allenmoos II* in Zurich. ↗ ⊠, ↗ *Architects Group Krokodil*

Roger Boltshauser

Boundaries ˈbaʊndrɪz, from the French *bordure*, originally 'border line', including Latin *limes* 'border'; in the legal sense a conceptual line that forms a border separating the territories of two states, an administrative boundary that delineates the areas of responsibility of authorities, or a municipal or district boundary that separates the areas administered by different local councils. The course followed by the boundary is determined by the regulations of international, constitutional, or administrative law and is physically marked by border signs. *(d3)* ↗ Setup Summer Academy, ↗ Studio B, H, ↗ *Island Subcities*, ↗ *Walled City*, ↗ Complementary to *International*

Brandlhuber, Arno Arno Brandlhuber, who was born in 1964, started working in various open and changing partnerships under the name *Brandlhuber+*. Brandlhuber holds the Chair for Architecture and Urban Research at the Academy of Fine Arts in Nuremberg and is initiator of the event *Akademie c/o* in Berlin, which understands architecture as the 'ordering of social relationships by built fabric' and represents a public platform for examining the 'spatial production of the Berlin Republic'. ↗ ⊠, ↗ Studio A, ↗ *Lecturer*

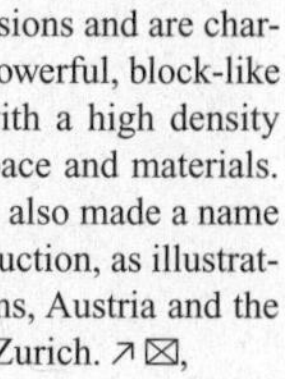
Arno Brandlhuber

Bridge **1.** brɪdʒ, from the Old High German *brucca*, related to the term *Prügel* (beating) originally from *Balken* (beam); a structure that brings transport routes, pipelines, etc., across or over natural or artificial barriers. A primary distinction is made between fixed and movable bridges, which in turn can be subdivided according to structural type, the kind of main beam used, the position of the carriageway, or according to the function or building material. *(b1/b30)* **2.** A bridge is a factory or device—usually a platform—used to connect two separate territories. To build a bridge: to create a physical or virtual relationship. *(md)* ↗ Studio C, D, ↗ *Autobahn Inhabited Bridges (AIB)*, ↗ *Infrastructure*

Brillembourg, Alfredo Alfredo Brillembourg, who was born in 1961 in New York, received his Bachelor of Art and Architecture in 1984 and his Master of Science in Architectural Design in 1986 from Columbia University. In 1992 he began his independent practice in architecture and one year later he founded *Urban-Think Tank (U-TT)* in Caracas, Venezuela and co-founded the *Sustainable Living Urban Model Laboratory (S.L.U.M. Lab)* with Hubert Klumpner. Since 2010, Brillembourg has held the chair for Architecture and Urban Design at the ETH Zurich. ↗ ⊠, ↗ Studio D, ↗ *Lecturer*, ↗ *Urban-Think Tank (U-TT)*

Alfredo Brillembourg

Building Typologies ˈbɪldɪŋ taɪˈpɒlədʒiːz; building or house typologies means the allocation of buildings to specific groups that differ according to their morphology or function. Building typology involves placing buildings in groups based on the distinctive characteristics of their architecture. The city, as a collection of very different individual structures, can be broken down according to these buildings: roughly into large and small, low and high, or very precisely into buildings with large or small windows. Identifying the characteristics of the various groups defines these different types and results in a catalogue that can provide a useful repertoire for an urban planning design. *(w)* ↗ *Hybrid Buildings*, ↗ *Typology Transfer*

C

Chemetoff, Alexandre Alexandre Chemetoff, who was born in 1950 in Paris, is an architect, urban planner, and landscape designer. He regards his work as a commitment, and has chosen to practice his activity in a free and open way by refusing to acknowledge the limits and borders between the disciplines. He perceives the practice of his profession as a multi-disciplinary art and sees the contemporary world as the content for the projects he undertakes and the actions he carries out. The program sets out the question, the site provides the resources, and the project a means of changing the rules of the game. ↗ ⊠, ↗ Incremental Masterplanning, ↗ *Lecturer*, ↗ *Panel Discussion*

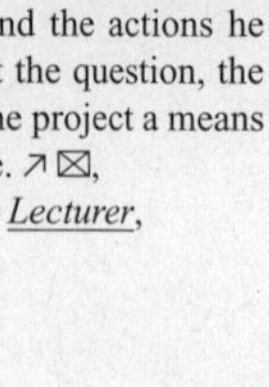
Alexandre Chemetoff

Chermayeff, Sam Sam Chermayeff, who was born in 1981 in New York, studied architecture at the University of Texas in Austin and the AA in London. He co-founded the office *June 14 Meyer-Grohbrügge & Chermayeff* in Berlin in 2001 after having worked for five years at *SANAA* in Tokyo. *June14* searches for an understanding of different ways of living and working in the contemporary world and therefore works on a wide range of projects. ↗ ⊠, ↗ Studio A, ↗ *Lecturer*

Sam Chermayeff

Christ & Gantenbein ↗ *Christ, Emanuel*, ↗ *Gantenbein, Christoph*

Christ, Emanuel Emanuel Christ, who was born in 1970, set up his practice *Christ & Gantenbein* in Basel together with Christoph Gantenbein, after graduating from the ETH Zurich in 1998. Together with six associates and a team of 35 architects, they work on a wide range of projects, including the renovation and extension of the Swiss National Museum in Zurich and the extension of the *Kunstmuseum* in Basel. Emanuel Christ has been a professor at the ETH Zurich since 2010. ↗ ⊠, ↗ Typology Transfer, ↗ *Christ & Gantenbein*, ↗ *Lecturer*, ↗ *Typology Transfer*

Emanuel Christ

City **1.** ˈsɪti, from Old French *cité*, from the Latin *cīvitās* 'a union of citizens', 'a citizenry'; a large settlement, bigger than a town. *(w)* **2.** Cities are communities with a population of at least 10,000. *(r)* **3.** Whereas the old city, which lay inside its fortifications, is symbolized by a boiled egg, the fried egg is used to represent the city between the 17th and 19th century. The metaphor for the highly complex nature of contemporary structures is the scrambled egg. *(Cedric Price, 1998)* ↗ ⊠

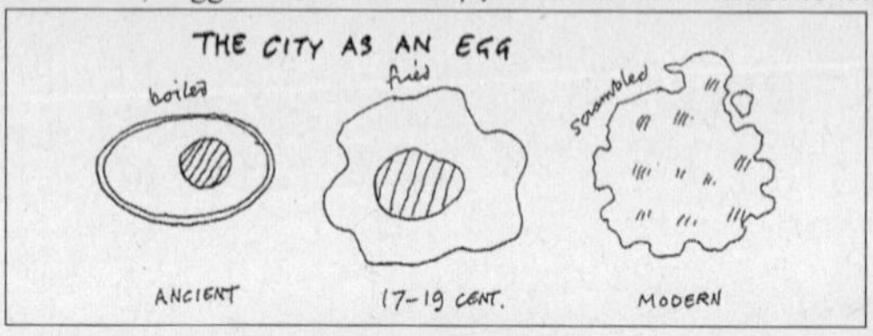

The city as an egg, by Cedric Price

City as Island ↗ *Archipelago*, ↗ *Island Subcities*

Coastline ˈkəʊstlaɪn; on the mainland the boundary of a coastal region to the water, on islands the border to the sand dunes and geest; delineates the area between the lowest tide level and the highest point on land that is reached by storm waves. *(b30)* ↗ Studio B, ↗ *Boundaries*

Collage **1.** ˈkɒlɑːʒ, from the French *papiers collés* 'glued picture', an image composed partly or entirely of pieces of pasted paper or other material. This technique, which was essentially not new, was introduced into modern art by Picasso, among others, as it was particularly well suited to the flat layout of images employed in synthetic cubism. The Futurists used the collage to achieve the kaleidoscopic, dynamic effects they aimed at. The Dadaists and Surrealists were interested primarily in the collage's surprise effect and in absurd combinations as well the playful outcome of chance. *(k)* **2.** Collaging: method of representing space. Method of producing space. Action and effect of using the collage technique to imagine a space or architectonic object. A substitute for sketches or working models. *(md)* ↗ *Collage City*, ↗ *Incremental Urbanism*

Collage City *Collage City*, a book written by Colin Rowe and Fred Koetter, proposes a city of fragments from the past, present, and future, taking inspiration from working examples in existing cities; some scientific, others picturesque; some antique, others contemporary; some may be rational, whilst others are disordered. Collage city would offer the poetics of Utopia, but the juxtaposition and layering of smaller designs into a whole (rather than a totalitarian, clean slate approach) would allow for the city to be free of the unchangeable finality of Utopian politics. A postmodern composition—lacking prescription—of remembrances, shifted contexts, recycled meanings, and metamorphoses … allowing the city to create itself, to read itself and to form its own meanings from borrowed fragments. *(ec)* ↗ ⊠, ↗ Mission Statement, ↗ Typology Transfer, ↗ Identity Markers …, ↗ Studio E, H, ↗ *Collage*

Community kəˈmjuːnɪtiː, from Latin *communitas*, from *commūnis* 'common'; a complex term that describes the relationship between people who are connected with each other on the basis of a historically developed religious-philosophical, political-ideological, theoretical, or narrowly defined purpose: a people, nation, state, church, (religious or political) community, marriage, family, friendship, organisation based on shared interests, association, and others. In sociology, a difference is drawn between society—a rationally constituted

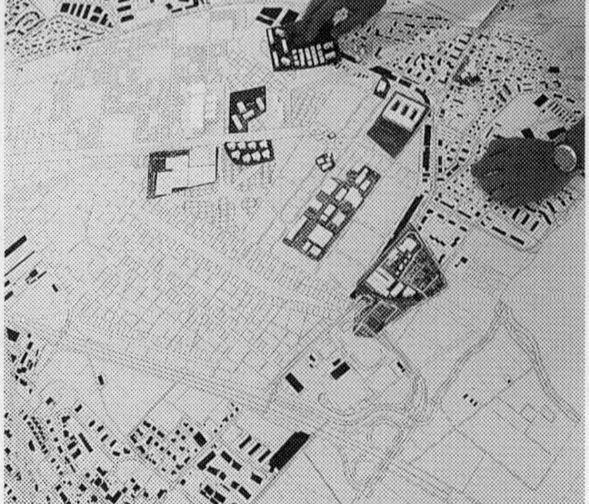
Working on a collage city

association on the basis of common interest—and community, which can be a group established on a natural basis or connected by shared ideas, but also a historically developed social association (e.g., village, old town). *(b15)* ↗ Identity Markers …, ↗ Studio D, ↗ *Networking*, ↗ *Responsibility*

Complementarity **1.** kɑmpləmenˈterəti, from the French *complémentaire*, from the Latin *complementum* 'completing', 'filling up'; harmonizing with each other, completing or rounding each other off. Describes the relationship between two terms that exclude but yet complete each other. *(d1)* **2.** Complementary characteristics belong together in as far as they refer to the same object. They exclude each other when they cannot meet spatially or temporally. As a rule two different qualities are involved, which, although not causally related, together produce a meaning. *(w)* **3.** In C. G. Jung's analytical psychology this relationship is called 'synchronicity'. In physics it is a phenomenon of quantum mechanics according to which certain complementary measurands cannot have a precisely defined value at the same time. ↗ Studio A, ↗ *Jung, C. G.*, ↗ *Pauli, Wolfgang*, ↗ *Audience / Lecturer*, ↗ *Boundaries / International*, ↗ *Incremental Urbanism / Tabula Rasa*

Context **1.** ˈkɒntekst, from the Latin *contextus* 'close connection', for instance 'the context (of a speech)', also *contexere* 'to link', 'weave together' **2.** *Context* is an essential architectural element because meaning can derive from context, as gestalt psychology emphasizes. *Context* is important because it acknowledges the quality of a place, of the whole beyond the single, and enhances an extended unity. *Context* does not mean the new has to look like the old—the old architectural vocabulary or urban composition or symbolic vocabulary. *(Venturi / Scott Brown, Architecture as Signs and Systems)* ↗ Identity Markers …, ↗ Résumé …

Crocodile (Krokodil) **1.** ˈkrɒkədaɪl; a reptile that lives in the water of which numerous different kinds exist; its name was borrowed in the 16th century from the Latin *crocodilus*, which is derived from the Greek *κροκόδειλος*. The Greek term initially described the lizard and actually means *gravel worm* (derived from *krókē* 'gravel' and *drîlos* 'worm'). *(d3)* **2.** A small crocodile made of clay, tied with strips of linen to the head and bearing the names of gods important for healing was used by the ancient Egyptians (c. 2500 BCE) for the non-medicinal treatment of headaches. By tightening the scalp, placing pressure on the widened blood vessels and cutting off the cranial arteries this method may well have been highly effective. ↗ ⊠⊠

Egyptian method of healing

D

Density **1.** ˈdensɪti; in general terms describes the quotient of a physical dimension and space, area, or length (spatial density, surface density, line density). **2.** Population density is the quotient of the population figure and an area of territory, generally given in inhabitants per square km. The population density is an expression of the intensity of settlement and a starting point for reflections about the capacity of a region or area. **3.** Development or building density is the relationship between the areas of a city that are built on and those without buildings. In the statistics, 'built' refers to the entire building plot. *(b15/b30)* **4.** You shall build densely. *(Manifesto by the Architects Group Krokodil)* **5.** Density per acre of ground assumes a quite different significance when we begin to pile dwelling units on top of one another and give up the amenity of the individual yard. *(Rem Koolhaas, S,M,L,XL)* ↗ Mission Statement, ↗ Studio H, G, ↗ *Island Subcities*, ↗ *Walled City*

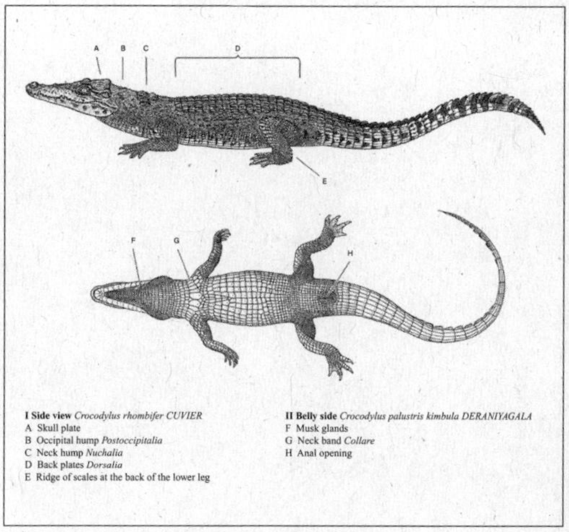

Principal characteristics of a crocodile

Dichotomy **1.** daɪˈkɒtəmi, from the Greek *dícha* 'separated', the two-part definition of a term by one subordinate to it and its negation, e.g., soul: the conscious, the unconscious. The dichotomy logically assumes the *tertium non datur* ('a third possibility is excluded'). In botany the term means a forked type of branching found in algae, mosses, and ferns. *(b30)* **2.** You shall consider city and country together. *(Manifesto by the Architects Group Krokodil)* **3.** Exterior / interior, public / private, geometric / shapeless, abstract / concrete, small / large, open / close, figure / ground, city / country: old dichotomies, for years paradigms of our disciplinary baggage, have suddenly lost their strict limits and yield new and effective binomials in interaction. Mixed 'coupled' realities, generated through unexpected associations and transversalities. *(md)* ↗ *Private / Public*, ↗ *City / Landscape*

Diener, Roger Roger Diener, who was born in 1950, is an architect and head of *Diener & Diener Architects*, Basel and Berlin. Having originally focused on residential projects, the firm now also systematically develops urban planning projects as well as projects for the renovation and extension of historic buildings. The basis of such designs is a perception of the European city in all its variety and continuity. Roger Diener is Professor of Architecture and Design at the ETH in Zurich. Together with Jacques Herzog, Pierre de Meuron and Marcel Meili, he heads the *ETH Studio Basel (Contemporary City Institute)*. ↗ ⊠, ↗ *ETH Studio Basel*, ↗ *Panel Discussion*

Roger Diener

Dietlikon *Municipality type:* work place community, *region:* Glatttal, *district:* Bülach, *post code:* 8305, *official municipality key:* 54, *population:* 7,097, *population density (inhabitants/km2):* 1,681.8, *height above sea level:* 445 m, *area (ha):* 422. *(st)* In 2008 the women of Dietlikon Unihockey Club became Swiss champions, cup-winners and European trophy winners. ↗ *Glatt—the City*

Dübendorf *Municipality type:* work place community, *region:* Glatttal, *district:* Uster, *post code:* 8600, *official municipality key:* 191, *population:* 25,124, *population density (inhabitants/km2):* 1,846, *height above sea level:* 440 m, *area (ha):* 1,361. *(st)* Dübendorf is the home of the Museum of the Swiss Air Force. ↗ *Glatt—the City*

Duchamp, Marcel French artist (1887–1968) whose work is most often associated with the Dadaist and Surrealist movements. Considered by some to be one of the most important artists of the 20th century, Duchamp's output influenced the development of Western art after World War I. Duchamp challenged conventional thinking about artistic processes and art marketing, not so much by writing, but through subversive actions. Duchamp produced relatively few artworks, while moving quickly through the avant-garde circles of his time. *(w)* ↗ 1m2/sec 08/15, ↗ *Abstraction*

E

Edler, Jan Jan Edler, who was born in 1970 in Cologne, studied architecture at Aachen University and the Bartlett School of Architecture in London. As part of the Berlin-based art group *Kunst und Technik* (1997–2000) he started to work with his brother Tim. In 2000 the brothers founded *realities:united* as a studio for art and architecture. Since then the Edlers, alias *realities:united*, have established a unique reputation for their spectacular art and media extensions to buildings by some of the world's most prominent figures in contemporary architecture. ↗ ⊠, ↗ *Lecturer*

Jan Edler

Eisinger, Angelus Angelus Eisinger, who was born in 1964, is an urban development and planning historian with a background in the social sciences and economics. In 2003, he completed his habilitation at the ETH Zurich. He has been Professor for history and culture of the metropolis at the Hafen City University in Hamburg since 2008. His research and teaching focus on the cultural aspects, as well as the impact of architecture, and town and regional development. Additionally, he works as a consultant and evaluator of planning

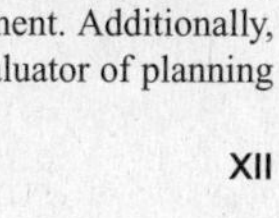

Angelus Eisinger

processes and participates in conceptual work for urban design competitions and planning studies. ↗ ⊠, ↗ Incremental Masterplanning, ↗ *Lecturer*, ↗ *Panel Discussion*

EM2N Architects ↗ *Hörmann, Fabian*, ↗ *Müller, Mathias*, ↗ *Niggli, Daniel*

ETH Studio Basel (Contemporary City Institute), ETH Studio Basel is an institute for urban research set up in Basel in 1999 by architects Roger Diener, Jacques Herzog, Marcel Meili, and Pierre de Meuron as part of the Swiss Federal Institute of Technology Zurich (ETH)—Department of Architecture, Network City and Landscape. ↗ *Diener, Roger*, ↗ *Meili, Marcel*

F

Fällanden *Municipality type:* affluent community, *region:* Glatttal, *district:* Uster, *post code:* 8117, *official municipality key:* 193, *population:* 8,062, *population density (inhabitants/km2):* 1,257.7, *height above sea level:* 459 m, *area (ha):* 641. (st) Fällanden is the end point of the 380 kV Sils-Fällanden power line that supplies the city of Zurich with electricity. ↗ *Glatt—the City*

First-August-Fireworks ↗ ⊠

Celebrating the Swiss National Holiday

Form **1.** ˈfɔːm, from Latin *forma* 'shape', 'figure', 'image', 'outline', 'plan', 'mould', 'frame', 'case'; describes the external shape, the outline, the growth or appearance of objects and living beings. The *architectural form* is the material result of architectural design. It is achieved through spatial, corporeal, and surface elements that fulfill a material and practical function and, above and beyond this, are shaped according to artistic standpoints. Together with the architectural content, the form makes up a dialectic entity. (a) **2.** Marc Angélil postulates *Form instead of Norm*, when he refers to the design potential of space: 08/15 urbanism needs to be radically changed, away from its anonymous conformity, towards the specific form of space. To represent the dimension of time he suggests marking the areas of the agglomeration with the colors red, green, and black. **3.** It is possible to direct the mental structuring of a city's image through form. The degree of clarity and legibility of form is made manifest in the ability of the user to recognize the parts and to synthesize a coherent whole. By choreographing the forms of a city, a designer is molding the identity of the place. Given the criteria of legibility, the language of form becomes highly important. (After Kevin Lynch) ↗ 1m2/sec 08/15, ↗ *Black*, ↗ *Green*, ↗ *Image*, ↗ *Morphology*, ↗ *Red*

Found Poem Do you think architecture is ...? *No.* What? *No.* Do you think architecture is ...? *No. No, I don't.* (Found at: www.a42.org) Inspired in part by Marcel Duchamp's readymades, Bern Porter (1911–2004) created poetry from mass-media images and verbiage that one might call a kind of alternative literature—package labels, banal instructions, lists. (David Byrne) Found poems, particularly ones of the mainstream variety, can seem like formalist exercises; for example, Howard Nemerov's *Found Poem* reorganizes language from *The St. Louis Post-Dispatch* into eight neatly arranged couplets. By contrast, Porter's approach was more visual and surprising and he focused less on poetically framing easily digestible information and more on creating strange and powerful hieroglyphs from the detritus of print culture. (w) ↗ *Duchamp, Marcel*

Frei, Raphael Raphael Frei, who was born in 1965, studied architecture at ETH Zurich. From 1997 he worked independently in the architects' cooperative *pool*, since 1998 he has been a partner in *pool Architects*. *pool Architects* arose out of a discussion forum assembling young practitioners in the field of urban planning. The office has won numerous competitions. They have realized a wide range of projects, from residential construction, school and office buildings to urban development. *pool Architects* taught at ETH Zurich as visiting professors. ↗ ⊠, ↗ *Architects Group Krokodil*, ↗ *pool Architects*

Raphael Frei

G

Gantenbein, Christoph Christoph Gantenbein, who was born in 1971, set up his practice *Christ & Gantenbein* in Basel together with Emanuel Christ, after graduating from the ETH Zurich in 1998. Together with six associates and a team of 35 architects, they work on a wide range of projects, including the renovation and extension of the Swiss National Museum in Zurich and the extension of the *Kunstmuseum* in Basel. Christoph Gantenbein has been a professor at ETH Zurich since 2010. ↗ ⊠, ↗ Typology Transfer, ↗ *Christ & Gantenbein*, ↗ *Lecturer*, ↗ *Typology Transfer*

Christoph Gantenbein

Girot, Christophe Christophe Girot, who was born in 1957, graduated with an M.Arch M.L.Arch from Berkeley. He is full professor at the Chair of Landscape Architecture at the Department of Architecture of the ETH Zurich, where he has been head of the Institute of Landscape Architecture since 2001. His research addresses three fundamental themes: new topological methods in landscape design, new media in landscape analysis and perception, and recent history and theory of landscape design. His professional practice at *Atelier Girot* focuses on large-scale landscape design. ↗ ⊠, ↗ Studio J, ↗ *Lecturer*

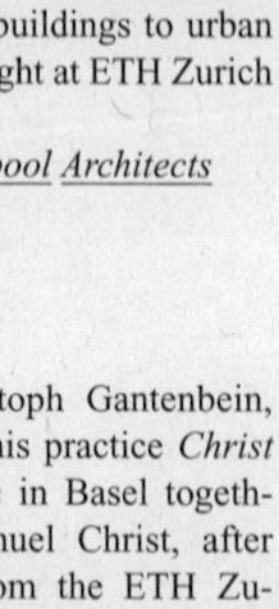

Christophe Girot

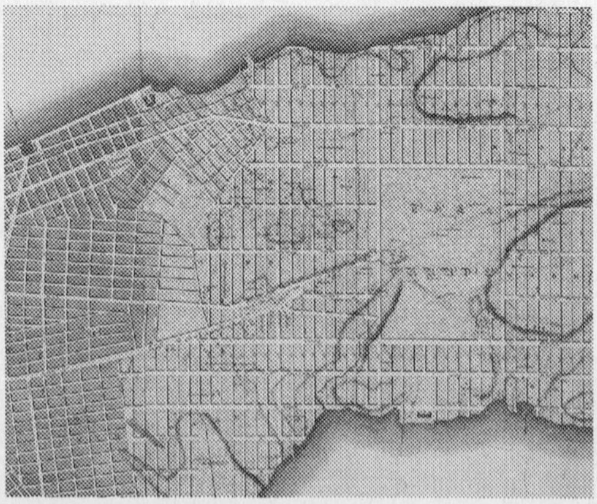

Intersection of the existing street plan with a proposed grid. New York, 1811, by W. Bridges

Glatt—the City **1.** Glatt is a city in progress; this means a city that does not yet know that it is one. The project by the Architects Group Krokodil *Glatt! Manifest für eine Stadt im Werden* (*Glatt! Manifesto for a City in Progress*) and the film *Glatt—the City* postulate this city in the Glatttal on the territory of the local communities. **2.** The new city of Glatt also called 'Glatttal city' is not based on the principle of the tabula rasa but follows an incremental logic. The existing and new are placed in a new relationship to each other and pieced together like in a collage. In an overall view, a vision develops of a dense, polycentric, urban, and sustainable city in the Glatttal. **3.** For the future planning of the 'Glatttal city', the Architects Group Krokodil authored a manifesto, designed a master plan, initiated a Summer Academy, and produced the film 'Glatt—the City'. The film tells of reporter Jean-Jacques Benoît being sent to Glatttal with the aim of questioning local residents about their new city. As soon as he arrives at the 'Glatt' shopping center the first problems emerge. Somehow or other the city is nowhere to be found and even the people he asks cannot really help the young journalist. The search for the new city begins. 2011, 08:57 min., directed by Chris Niemeyer, *planB Films*. ↗ Mission Statement, ↗ *Architects Group Krokodil*, ↗ *Benoît, Jean-Jacques*

Glätttal **1.** The Glatttal (spelled Glattal until 1998) also 'Glatt valley' is a region to the north of the city of Zurich in the Swiss Canton Zurich. It encompasses the area between the Greifensee and Glattfelden through which the River Glatt, a tributary of the Rhine, flows. Glatttal is a typical Zwischenstadt or intermediate city (Thomas Sieverts), an agglomeration landscape between city and country. (w/ag) **2.** Figures on the Glatttal: *total area:* 12,885 ha, *settlement area:* 36.6 %, *population 2011:* 156,106, *population growth 2001–2011:* 18 %, *65-years old and older:* 15.6 %, *average age:* 40.5, *in employment:* 118,077, *newly created dwellings:* 870, *local coefficient of taxation:* 98.6 %, *taxation capacity:* 3,626 Fr./resident. (w/st) ↗ *Glatt—the City*, ↗ *Zwischenstadt*

Görlich, Ulrich ↗ Schlieren, ↗ *Lecturer*, ↗ *Long-Term Photographic Observation* ...

Green **1.** griːn, from the Dutch and Old German *gruoen/grün* 'to grow, turn green', originally 'grass colored', 'related to grass'. *(d1)* Describes the color sensation created by light with a wave length between around 490 and 560 nm or by the subtractive mixing of the two primary colors cyan blue and yellow. In the symbolism of color green, as it comes from the awakening of nature, represents hope and cheerfulness, in medieval courtly love poetry the start of a new love. Green is the color of Islam (it was Mohammed's favorite color) and is found in the flags of a number of Islamic states. In the late 18th century green was the color of freedom, in the 20th century it became the symbol of environmental protection organizations. *(b30)* **2.** In the lecture of Marc Angélil, green stands for unbuilt matter or nature. ↗1m2/sec 08/15, ↗Black, ↗Red

Greifensee Municipality type: suburban residential community, region: Glatttal, district: Uster, post code: 8606, official municipality key: 194, population: 5,122, population density (inhabitants/km2): 2198.3, height above sea level: 443 m, area (ha): 233. *(st)* Located on the lake of the same name. Because the oxygen content of the Greifensee Lake is often too low in the summer months, a lake water ventilation plant was installed in 2009. ↗Glatt—the City

Grid **1.** ˈgrɪd, from an abbreviation of *griddle* or *gridiron*. A rectangular array of squares or rectangles of equal size. A 'grid plan' is a method of city and regional planning in which streets and administrative units are arranged at right angles. *(w)* **2.** The grid—or any other subdivision of the metropolitan territory into maximum increments of control—describes an archipelago of 'cities within cities'. The more each 'island' celebrates different values, the more the unity of the archipelago as a system is reinforced. Because 'change' is contained in the component 'islands', such a system will never have to be revised. *(Rem Koolhaas)* ↗⊠, ↗Abstraction, ↗Archipelago, ↗Planning

Group picture ↗⊠⊠

Studio I

Studio J

H

Heller, Martin Martin Heller, who was born in 1952, founded *Heller Enterprises* in 2003 and since then has worked as an independent exhibition curator, author, and cultural entrepreneur on several projects in Switzerland, Germany, and Austria. He has served as director of the Museum of Design in Zurich, artistic director of the Swiss national exhibition *Expo.02*, and artistic director of *Linz 2009 European Capital of Culture*. He was involved in the concept development of the *International Building Exhibition (IBA)* in 2020. Martin Heller is currently responsible for planning the content of the future *Humboldt Forum* in Berlin. ↗⊠, ↗Panel Discussion

Martin Heller

Hörmann, Fabian Fabian Hörmann, who was born in 1978 in Bielefeld / Germany, studied architecture in Stuttgart and Las Palmas and worked in the fields of film, media, and architecture in Germany, The Netherlands, and Switzerland. From 2001 to 2002 and from 2004 to 2006 he worked at *EM2N Architects* before running his own architectural practice *BEACH* and co-founding the cultural platform *FC Hinterhof* in Stuttgart. In 2008 he became an associate on *EM2N*'s management board, heading the competition and design department. In 2010 he co-founded the alternative rock band *GRAN NOIR*. ↗⊠, ↗EM2N Architects, ↗Architects Group Krokodil

Fabian Hörmann

Hybrid Buildings **1.** ˈhaɪbrɪd ˈbɪldɪŋz, 'hybrid' (adjective) from Latin *hybrida*, a variant of *ibrida* 'a mongrel'; specifically, offspring of a tame sow and a wild boar. 'Building' (noun) is meant as any human-made structure used or intended for supporting or sheltering any use or continuous occupancy. *(w)* **2.** Buildings are generally registered and classified according to their function. In the case of hybrid buildings this system cannot be so easily applied, as at least two or more functions are conceivable. Building functions are thus often mixed and may change over the course of time. In the modern city the function of a building has changed from the homogeneous to the heterogeneous. The increasing density of cities and the development of building technologies have encouraged a mix of functions, despite opinions that a building should look how it is. In hybrid buildings the form can remain the same while the function changes. The important thing is that a modern building should be able to deal with changes of function. *(Adapted from Steven Holl's Alphabetical City)* ↗⊠, ↗Autobahn Inhabited Bridges (AIB), ↗Building Typologies

I

Ideal City aɪˈdɪəl ˈsɪti; complexes planned according to utopian or ideal concepts, generally only partly realized. The starting point is provided by theoretical concepts about the character of a social system, often, however, the concept later fails when it encounters the objective rules of development. Designs of this kind extend from Plato and Aristotle, to Vitruvius, Alberti, and Filarete right up to the era of modernism with the idea of the garden city and postmodernism with Le Corbusier's *Ville Radieuse* or Richard Neutra's *Rush-City-Project* (as examples). ↗⊠, ↗Book chapter Software, ↗City, ↗Non-Place

Ville Radieuse: Le Corbusier's ideal city

Identity **1.** aɪˈdentɪti, from the late Latin *identitas*, the Latin *idem* 'the same'; *a)* the genuine nature of a person or thing; complete agreement with what it is or what it is described as; *b)* (psychology) the inner unity of the person experienced as the 'self': finding, searching for one's identity; *c)* (no plural) complete agreement with someone in relation to something; sameness. *(d1)* **2.** A dilemma always associated with urban change is that it destroys points

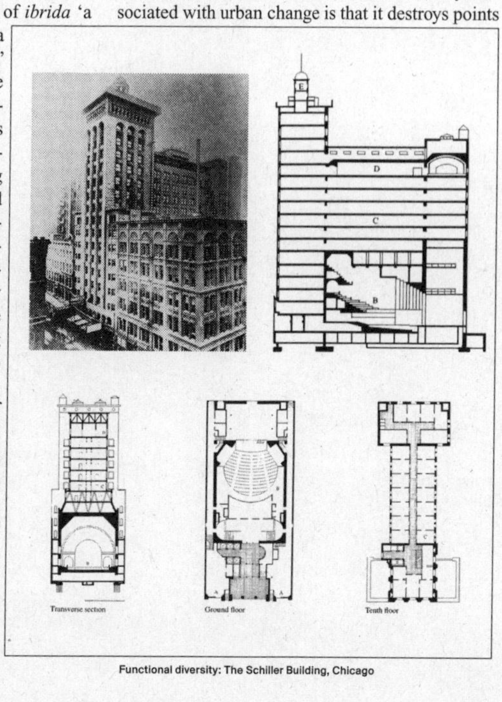

Functional diversity: The Schiller Building, Chicago

of identity within the urban landscape and thus demands mental adaptation to the changing images of the city from its inhabitants. The willingness of the observers to identify with the city and its places is, alongside their knowledge and the visual elements (forms), essential for the image of the city. *(After Kevin Lynch)* **3.** Identity and ecological quality of a landscape can really add value to the mosaic of locations, which in the end makes the metropolitan region of Zurich work, like any urban region. *(Markus Schaefer)* **4.** You shall create a sense of identity. *(Manifesto by the Architects Group Krokodil)*
↗ Mission Statement, ↗ Identity Markers …,
↗ *Image*

Image **1.** ˈɪmɪdʒ, from the Greek *eikon*, *eidolon*; Latin *imago*; the term is used to describe: *a)* representational artifacts on a surface, such as paintings, drawings etc., *b)* metaphysical archetype—copy relationships, *c)* natural images, such as reflections, shadows or imprints, *d)* inner images (imagined images, dream images, etc.), and *e)* linguistic images (comparisons, metaphors). *(b15/b30)* **2.** For Kevin Lynch, the 'imageability' of a city is directly related to the success of its urban plan. His study in *The Image of the City* focuses on the components of a city (path, edge, district, node, and landmark) that are used to build order into its structure. ↗ *City*

Imitation **1.** ˌɪmɪˈteɪʃn̩, from the Latin *imitatio* 'copy'; means the imitation of something, for instance, birds' voices, or the copying of an object. *(b15)* Imitation is also produced as an effect using an electronic echo device. **2.** Identification and imitation can only be distinguished from each other when a person is conscious of his imitations. *(d1)*
↗ ☒, ↗ *Ideal City*

Imitation

Incremental Urbanism **1.** ˌɪnkrəˈmentl̩ ˈɜːbəˌnɪzm, 'Incremental' (adjective): from the Latin *incrementum*, 'growth', 'increase'; taking place in stages, building one upon the other. 'Urbanism' (noun): from the Latin *urbs* 'city' and *urbanus* 'belonging to the city'; characteristic of the city, of city life. *(d1)* **2.** At a time when territory is occupied in an increasingly hypertrophic way, the all-embracing master plan seems increasingly limited. Incremental urbanism means the specific implementation of an idea which, although originally abstract, is nevertheless anchored in the concrete circumstances of the place: *A novel contribution to a specific urban environment (Angelus Eisinger)*. It is a strategy of growing structures built upon each other, historical and referential, which functions as hybrid approach between *top-down* and *bottom-up*. Incremental urbanism contrasts with the master plan, which functions independently of the place. It does not mean the radical change of space on the basis of ideal concepts and utopias, i.e., decidedly not the tabula rasa. **3.** Urbanism will never again be about the new, only about the more and the modified. *(Rem Koolhaas, What Ever Happened to Urbanism?)*
↗ Mission Statement, ↗ Incremental Masterplanning, ↗ *Context*, ↗ *Ideal City*, ↗ *Palimpsest*,
↗ Complementary to *Tabula Rasa*

Infrastructure **1.** ˈɪnfrəstrʌktʃə, from latin *infra* 'below' and *structura* 'adjustment', 'building', 'erection', 'a building', 'edifice', 'structure'; a difference is drawn between personal infrastructure (the intellectual, entrepreneurial abilities, and craftsmanship of persons involved in the economic process, human capital), institutional infrastructure (social norms and behavior patterns, facilities and processes) and material infrastructure ('social overhead capital'). The latter, which includes all the state and private facilities on which the economic development of a society of a region is based and is divided into technical infrastructure and social infrastructure. *(lw)* **2.** The city and its infrastructure, the infrastructure and its city. One determines the other. They interact dialectically. Cities are inseparably linked with their infrastructures. Accordingly, urban planning must deal with the built and spatial design of urban structures, their functions and control. **3.** Communication and transport infrastructures emerge as the most evident lines of the current 'urban-territorial' system. Lines are converted into neutral directories for the future organisation of the land. *(md)* ↗ Book chapter Networking, ↗ Studio C, D, F, I, J, ↗ *Bridge*, ↗ *Mobility*,
↗ *Networking*

International **1.** ˌɪntəˈnæʃn̩əl, from *inter-* 'among', 'between', 'amid' and *national* 'having to do with a nation'; *a)* of, relating to, or involving two or more nations, *b)* extending across or transcending national boundaries. **2.** The students and lecturers at the International Summer Academy Zurich came from 5 continents, 29 countries, and from 77 different towns and cities.
↗ ☒

Intervention ˌɪntəˈvenʃn̩, from the late Latin *interventio* 'mediation', 'involvement', '(controlling) intervention'. In the 17th century, German borrowed the verb *intervenieren* as a political term from the French word *intervenir*. This comes from the Latin *intervenire* 'to step between', 'to come between' (cf. Advent). *(b15)* ↗ Setup Summer Academy, ↗ Incremental Masterplanning

Island Subcities **1.** ˈaɪlənd sʌbˈsɪtɪz; reading the city as a group of islands means assuming autonomous systems within the greater entity. These 'island subcities' are isolated, high density urban districts with clear, 'hard' boundaries that separate them from their unprogrammatic surroundings. **2.** In Mark Lee's Summer Academy Studio, the archipelago or the island city provides a basis supposition that appears in four forms: as a triangle, a rectangle, a pentagon, and a circle—each form allotted a particular program. These four urban figures are positioned in the Glatttal in a deliberate and focused way. **3.** Island-(sub)cities are new settlements in the territory that institute a new use in the territory, such as leisure centers, business parks, shopping complexes, residential areas, … All the functions generated by these island-cities are the same as those of traditional cities. They are cities within cities. *(md)* ↗ Studio G,
↗ *Archipelago*, ↗ *Autonomous Urbanism*

J

Jung, C. G. Swiss psychiatrist who was born in 1875 in Kesswil / Bodensee, and died in 1962 in Küsnacht. Along with Sigmund Freud and Alfred Adler, Carl Gustav Jung was one of the pioneers of psychoanalysis. As a student of Freud he promoted and expanded his teacher's work in the area of psychoanalysis, but after 1912 Jung turned away from Freud and developed his own form of analytical psychology at the center of which he placed the collective unconscious. *(h)* ↗ Studio A,
↗ *Synchronicity*

K

Kloten *Municpality type:* work place community, *region:* Glatttal, *district:* Bülach, *post code:* 8302, *official municipality key:* 62, *population:* 18,183, *population density (inhabitants/km2):* 942.1, *height above sea level:* 447m, *area (ha):* 1,930. In 2009 the town of Kloten was awarded the label 'Energy City' for its sustainable and efficient energy policy. *(st)* ↗ *Glatt—the City*

Klumpner, Hubert Hubert Klumpner, who was born in 1965 in Salzburg, graduated in 1993 from the University of Applied Arts in Vienna. Klumpner later worked with Enrique Miralles and Paul Rudolph before receiving a Master of Science in Architecture and Urban Design from Columbia University in 1997. In 1998 Klumpner joined Alfredo Brillembourg as Director of *Urban-Think Tank (U-TT)* in Caracas and co-founded the *Sustainable Living Urban Model Laboratory (S.L.U.M. Lab)*. Since 2010, Klumpner has held the chair for Architecture and Urban Design at the ETH in Zurich. ↗ ☒, ↗ Studio D, ↗ *Urban-Think Tank (U-TT)*, ↗ *Lecturer*

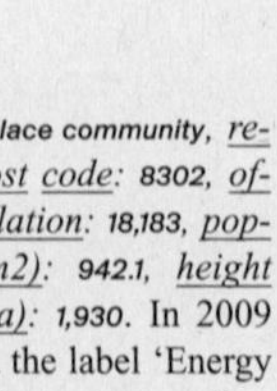

Hubert Klumpner

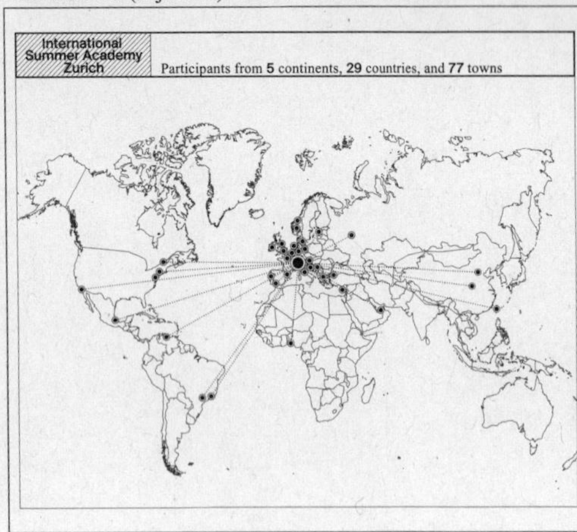

Participants came from all over the world

L

Emanuel Christ, Summer Academy Lecturer

Freek Persyn, Summer Academy Lecturer

Christophe Girot, Summer Academy Lecturer

Landscape **1.** ˈlændskeɪp, from an alteration of earlier *landskip*, *lantschip* (derived from Dutch *landschap*), from Old English *landscipe*, *landsceap* 'region', 'district', 'tract of land'; region or area of territory, a region regarded as a single entity or assessed as such. *(b30)* In aesthetic or symbolic terms stands for the result or content of a culturally-shaped subjective visual perception of a region as a harmonious entity. In geographical terms it means a part of the earth with a uniform impact and appearance. *(w)* **2.** Landscape can be taken as an anchor of identity that helps orchestrate and structure peripheral growth *(Studio J)*, or/and as starting point, because landscape is a useful organizational element in cities that are not densely packed *(Studio I)*. As Markus Schaefer summarizes, landscape is a powerful tool for organizing territory. *(Résumé)* However, landscape can be used not only as a conceptual instrument, but also as goal, as a vision. For example in the form of an idyllic life in a green landscape *(Studio B)*. **3.** Much more than a former model, landscape is important to architecture and urbanism as a model of process. Landscapes cannot be designed and controlled to the degree that architecture is; instead, landscapes, like cities, are loosely structured frameworks that grow in and change over time. Landscapes are immersive environments, diagrams subject to only partial control. *(md)* ↗ Book chapter Landscape, ↗ Studio B, I, J, ↗ Résumé …, ↗ *Scales of Water*

Lecture ˈlektʃə, from Latin *lectus*, past participle of *legō* 'I read', 'I recite'; means *a)* lecture, treatise on a certain theme, *b)* a berating or scolding. *(b30)*

Lecturer **1.** ˈlektʃərə, for etymology see 'Lecture'; means *a)* someone who gives a lecture, speaker, *b)* A member of a university below the rank of assistant or associate professor. *(b30/w)* **2.** 31 lecturers gave talks during the Summer Academy. ↗ ⊠ ⊠ ⊠, ↗ *Lecture*

Lee, Mark Mark Lee, who was born in 1967, is the principal of *Johnston Marklee & Associates*. The Los Angeles based firm has been engaged in a range of commissions in the U.S., Europe, and South America since 1998 and has received several awards. Combining his academic and design expertise, Mark Lee conducts speculative research based on critical reassessments of architectural and urban design history and has written and lectured widely on his research. Mark Lee has taught at the ETH Zurich, the TU Berlin, and at the University of California. ↗ ⊠, ↗ Studio G, ↗ *Lecturer*

Mark Lee

Leeser, Jörg Jörg Leeser, who was born in 1967, worked as an architect in New York and Cologne, as assistant professor in New York, and at RWTH Aachen University. Since 2007 he has been teaching as a professor at the Bergische University Wuppertal and presently teaches also at the Peter Behrens School of Architecture in Düsseldorf. In 2000, he and Anne-Julchen Bernhardt established *BeL Associates*. They have received numerous awards. The office has worked on 95 projects, of which 15 have been completed. ↗ ⊠, ↗ Studio E, ↗ *BeL Associates*, ↗ *Lecturer*

Jörg Leeser

Long-Term Photographic Observation of Schlieren 2005–2020 The research project at Zurich University of the Arts follows the urban development of Schlieren over a period of 15 years by means of long-term photographic documentation. The photographic long-term observation by Meret Wandeler and Ulrich Görlich aims at showing the impact of measures for sustainable urban development and improving the quality of life and identity suggested in the urban development concept. The project is organized as a case study. Using the example of Schlieren, it develops exemplary photographical methods for the visualization of special development processes in the agglomeration. ↗ Schlieren, ↗ *Agglomeration*, ↗ *Görlich, Ulrich*, ↗ *Wandeler, Meret*

City metaphors: Protection, symbolized by a morphological relationship (O. M. Ungers)

M

Master Plan **1.** ˈmɑːstə plæn, from Latin *magister* 'chief', 'teacher' and *planus* 'flat', 'plane'; *a)* a comprehensive document that sets out an overall strategy, *b)* a small-scale graphic outline that shows all the major elements of a project, *c)* an overall, comprehensive plan, a concept for action with goals for implementing visions and a number of individual projects derived from them. *(w)* **2.** According to Angelus Eisinger the master plan promises to undertake the systematic ordering of entire cities or entire urban districts, then to meticulously give the elements of this order a greater depth and, finally, to implement it, plot by plot, ensemble by ensemble—always in accordance with the stipulations of the overriding idea. ↗ Incremental Masterplanning, ↗ *Ideal City*, ↗ *Planning*

Meili, Marcel Marcel Meili, who was born in 1953, set up *Meili, Peter Architects* together with Markus Peter in 1987. Their recent built work includes the Zurich Central Station extension, *Klanghaus* Toggenburg, the *Zollfreilager* Zurich, and *Sprengel Museum* Hanover. Marcel Meili was a lecturer at the International Summer Academy Berlin in 1987, and taught as visiting professor at the Harvard Graduate School of Design. Since 1999 he has been teaching as a professor at the ETH Zurich where—together with Jacques Herzog, Pierre de Meuron, Roger Diener, and Christian Schmid—he founded and runs *ETH Studio Basel (Contemporary City Institute)*. ↗ ⊠, ↗ *ETH Studio Basel*, ↗ *Panel Discussion*

Marcel Meili

Mobility **1.** məʊˈbɪlɪti, from the Latin *mobilitas* 'moveability' generally means the movement of people in social spaces and/or their spatial and regional mobility, but also their intellectual flexibility. A difference is drawn between, for example, spatial movement processes and movement within the social structures of a society (social mobility). High levels of mobility are a characteristic of dynamic industrialized societies. *(ws)* **2.** The recognition of the factor 'mobility' questions the simple description of a city as a place with large numbers of people and a collection of buildings. *(ws)* ↗ Studio D, F

Morphology **1.** mɔːˈfɒlədʒi, from the Greek *morphé* 'shape', 'form' and *lógos* 'word', 'theory', 'reason'; is the theory of form. The term 'morphology' was coined by Johann Wolfgang Goethe and established as a science 'which is intended to record both the special and also the general structural laws of objects dealt with by other sciences'.

2. O. M. Ungers used this term in the *morphological design concept*, which he helped to shape: the perception of the environment demands an interpretation in a morphological sense that is wide open to subjective speculations and transformations. It is an interpretation on a conceptual level, which shows ideas, notions, metaphors, and analogies, and embeds transcendental aspects in an overriding context. According to Ungers, this is the only way in which the whole can be registered as more than is represented by the sum of its parts. It transcends the pure analysis of a series of things, as this cannot grasp their characteristics. ↗ ⊠, ↗ Analysis, ↗ Form, ↗ Image, ↗ Ungers, O. M., ↗ Walled City

Müller, Mathias Mathias Müller, who was born in 1966, studied architecture at ETH Zurich. In 1998 he set up the office *EM2N Architects* together with Daniel Niggli. *EM2N* works on a wide variety of assignments ranging from housing to public, educational and sports buildings, infrastructure and city planning. Their projects are located in Switzerland, France, Czech Republic, the Ukraine, and China. In addition to a number of building awards they have received the *Swiss Art Award* in architecture. Mathias Müller and Daniel Niggli have been visiting professors at the EPFL, as well as ETH Zurich. ↗ ⊠, ↗ Architects Group Krokodil, ↗ EM2N Architects

Mathias Müller

Murphy, Don Don Murphy, who was born in 1965, studied at Southbank University London and was one of the first graduates of the Berlage Institute. In 1995 he established *VMX Architects* together with Leon Teunissen in Amsterdam. The projects by *VMX* range from the design of a table to the design of a temporary bicycle storage facility, and from the complete modification of an existing house to the design of large, complex public buildings, hospitals, offices, and schools. Don Murphy has lectured at various universities. ↗ ⊠, ↗ Studio B ↗ Lecturer

Don Murphy

N

Networking 1. ˈnetwɜːkɪŋ; means the art of establishing and cultivating a network. *(we)* **2.** Networking is a system consisting of individual parts that are linked with each other in a variety of ways through cause and effect relationships and general and particular system characteristics. In visual terms we speak of a 'network of relationships'. *(w)* Different systems within the city, for example the traffic system or individual districts, are structurally coupled with each other and with the city. ↗ ⊠, ↗ Book chapter Networking, ↗ Studio D, F, ↗ Bridge, ↗ Community, ↗ Mobility

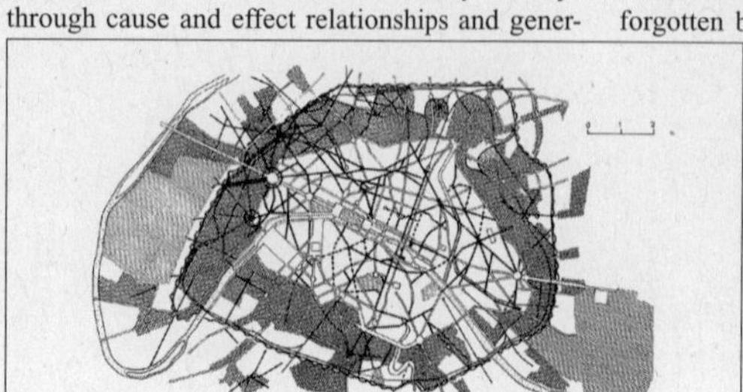

Baron Georges-Eugène Haussmann, plan of Paris, 1853

Niggli, Daniel Daniel Niggli, who was born in 1970, studied architecture at ETH Zurich. Together with Mathias Müller he set up the office *EM2N Architects* in 1998. *EM2N* works on a wide variety of assignments ranging from housing to public, educational and sports buildings, infrastructural and city planning. Their projects are located in Switzerland, France, Czech Republic, the Ukraine, and China. In addition to a number of building awards they have received the *Swiss Art Award* in architecture. Mathias Müller and Daniel Niggli have been visiting professors at the EPFL, as well as at ETH Zurich. ↗ ⊠, ↗ Architects Group Krokodil, ↗ EM2N Architects

Daniel Niggli

Non-Place 1. nɒn-ˈpleɪs, related to 'Utopia', from the Greek *ou* 'not' and *tópos* 'place', 'point', 'land', therefore actually 'the non-land', 'nowhere', or the 'non-place'; a land that does not really exist but is only imagined in which ideal social conditions exist. In the work by the English humanist, Thomas More (ca. 1478–1535), Utopia is an island country with 54 cities, elected representatives, and a president who holds office for life. The people live entirely from farming. Daily life and social life are unanimously agreed upon, monogamy is dominant, but divorce is possible by mutual agreement under state supervision. In their leisure time the Utopians devote themselves to humanist education. The people practice a religion of reason with unelaborate rituals and prayers that are phrased in such a way that all individuals can relate to themselves that which everybody says simultaneously.' *(d1/bk)* **2.** The term 'non-place' offers a suggestion about a new relationship between time-city and space of mobility. The non-places identified by Marc Augé are: office parks, stations, motorways, camp sites and caravan parks, airports and railway stations, hotel chains and shopping malls, structures for leisure and even telecommunication networks. They constitute new paradigms for everyday scenarios which are 'architecturalized' and, at the same time, forgotten by the culture of architecture. *(md/Marc Angé, Places and Non-Places)* ↗ Ideal City

Norm ↗ Form

O

Oerlikon, (Neu-) Oerlikon, once an independent political community in Canton Zurich, was incorporated in the City of Zurich in 1934. Since the 1990s, a new urban district has been developing to the northwest of the railway station (including Oerliker Park 2001). This district forms the link between the city of Zurich and the urban growth region Glatttal city *(cf. Historical Dictionary of Switzerland)*. Neu-Oerlikon is one of the largest inner city urban development areas in Switzerland. The cantonal center for vocational guidance is located in Oerlikon. ↗ Glatt—the City

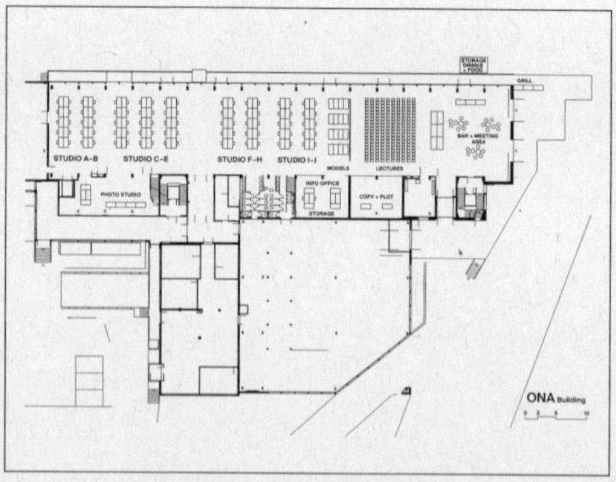

Venue of the Summer Academy 2012 in Oerlikon, Zurich

ONA Building ↗ ⊠, ↗ Oerlikon, (Neu-)

Opfikon Municipality type: workplace community, region: Glatttal, district: Bülach, post code: 8152, official municipality key: 66, population: 15,967, population density (inhabitants/km2): 2,846.2, height above sea level: 455 m, area (ha): 561. The editorial office of the motor-bike magazine *Moto Sport Schweiz* is located in an area of Opfikon known as Glattbrugg. *(st)* ↗ Glatt—the City

P

Paella Ingredients for paella: 6 boneless chicken breasts or thighs, preferably free-range or organic, skin left on, each quartered; sea salt and freshly ground black pepper; plain flour for dusting; olive oil; 100 g chorizo, sliced; 6 slices pancetta or streaky bacon; 1 onion, finely chopped; 4 cloves of garlic, finely chopped; 2 liters hot chicken stock, preferably organic; 2 large pinches of saffron; 1 heaped teaspoon smoked paprika; 500 g paella rice; small bunch flat leaf parsley, leaves picked and chopped, stalks chopped; 2 handfuls peas, fresh or frozen; 10 king prawns; optional: 500 g mussels, scrubbed; optional: 2 small squids, halved and scored. ↗ ⊠, ↗ Studio A

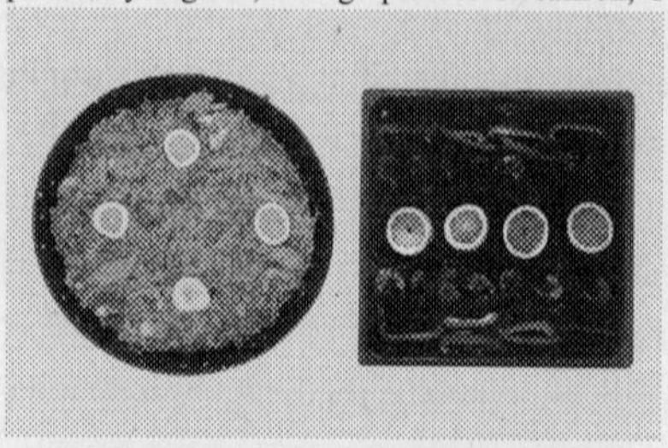

Learning from the circled and the squared ↗ in analogy to pp. 96–97

Palimpsest 1. ˈpælɪmpsest, from the Greek *palimpsēstos*, actually 'scratched off again', in Latin Codex *rescriptus* 'manuscript written over again'. Manuscript from which the original writing was removed—by wiping it off papyrus or erasing it with a pumice stone from parchment—and replaced by more recent writing. Reusing expensive writing materials was standard practice among the Romans, as it was in the monastic *scriptoria* of the early Middle Ages. There are only few surviving palimpsests from the post-Carolingian era. Fluorescent photography is a modern aid in deciphering palimpsests. *(b30)* **2.** André Corboz suggests reading the city as a palimpsest *(The Territory as a Palimpsest, 2001)* i.e. 'no longer understanding the territory as a quasi-abstract field of activity but as the result of an extremely lengthy and very gradual accumulation of layers, which one ought to be aware

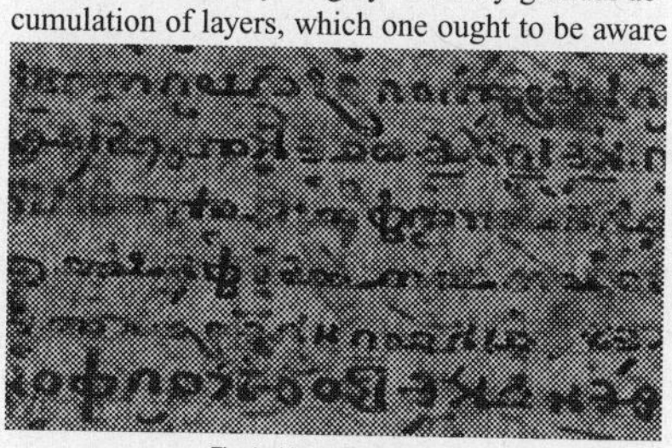

The Archimedes palimpsest

of before intervening in it. ... Most of these layers are very thin and also full of holes. Above all one does not only add something to them but rather erases something. ... The territory, which is completely permeated by traces and violent attempts at reading it, resembles most closely a palimpsest.' **3.** The possibility of inscribing time in space. Complementary to a *tabula rasa* strategy. ↗⊠, ↗1m2/sec 08/15, ↗*Incremental Urbanism*

Panel Discussion **1.** ˈpænḷ dɪˈskʌʃṇ, from the Old French *panel*, today *panneau* 'board', 'panel', and from the Latin *discutere*, 'to refute'. At a panel discussion or conversation, experts or representatives of interest groups come together in front of a larger audience, in order to present their opinions, to compare them and in this way to arrive jointly at an added value. **2.** Panel discussion at the Summer Academy on the theme 'Incremental Urbanism' on July 25, 2012 chaired by Angelus Eisinger, with

Panel discussion

Martin Heller, Alexandre Chemetoff, and Marcel Meili

Alexandre Chemetoff, Marcel Meili, Roger Diener, and Martin Heller. ↗⊠⊠, ↗Incremental Masterplanning, ↗*Eisinger, Angelus*

Pauli, Wolfgang Swiss-American physicist of Austrian origin who was born in 1900 in Vienna and died in 1958 in Zurich. Studied physics at Munich University, from 1928 Professor for Theoretical Physics at the ETH Zurich. From 1935–36 and 1940–45 he was visiting professor at Princeton / New Jersey, USA. Pauli was one of the leading physicists of the 20th century who, above all with his contribution to quantum mechanics and quantum field theory, carried out highly important work. Pauli was a patient of C. G. Jung and the correspondence between them has been published in book form. ↗Studio A, ↗*Jung, C. G.*, ↗*Complementarity*

Performance **1.** pəˈfɔːməns; term for a process-oriented art form in which the actual work is replaced by artistic action in front of a public. *(b15)* **2.** Of all conceptual paradigms of architecture, performance is the one that seeks to evaluate the efficiency of its ambitions. Opposed to an architecture for the sake of architecture, it investigates the feed-back loops between architecture and the system it is embedded in. Isolated questions of form, process, fabrication, etc. cease to be a priori conditions of architecture. Performance does not ask what a form looks like, but what it enables. It does not focus on what process was used to make the design, but on what the process was able to generate in the design. Thus performance shifts the focus of interest from essence to effect. The question is not what something is, but what it does. *(Andreas Ruby)* ↗Just Imagine a City is Made ..., ↗*Paper Performance*

Paper Performance ↗⊠

Performing the Summer Academy newspaper during the final reviews

Periphery **1.** pəˈrɪfəriː, from the Ancient Greek *περιφέρεια*, *periphereia*, 'the line around the circle', 'circumference', 'part of a circle', 'an arc', 'the outer surface'; edge area, edge zone, surrounding line (in particular of a circle), edge district, urban outskirts. The verb on which it is based, *periphérein* 'to carry around', is formed from *phérein* 'to carry', 'to bring'. *(d3)* **2.** Today the periphery is neither scenario nor model—a referential landscape—but rather, an open situation, to be qualified on the basis of restructuring strategies. Re-informers of the city and of the territory. *(md)* ↗*Landscape*, ↗*Suburb*

Persyn, Freek Not long after graduating from the Sint-Lucas School of Architecture in Brussels, Freek Persyn, born in 1974, jointly founded the practice of *51N4E* with Peter Swinnen and Johan Anrys. Until 2003, one year before *51N4E* was awarded the Rotterdam Maaskant Award for Young Architects, he also freelanced for *Xaveer de Geyter Architects*. Parallel to running his studio, Persyn has been involved in the academic field as assistant professor at the University of Gent and currently as visiting professor at the Academy of Architecture in Mendrisio, Switzerland. ↗⊠, ↗*Lecturer*

Freek Persyn

Planning **1.** ˈplænɪŋ; means mentally anticipating the means and steps, along with their sequence, which appear necessary to successfully achieve a goal. In the more comprehensive sense, planning means the intellectually and later organizationally and institutionally formed process of determining by means of estimates, designs, and decisions along which paths, through which steps, in which temporal and organizational order, under which circumstances and, finally, for what costs and with which consequences a goal appears achievable. *(b15)* **2.** I find it interesting to understand the city no longer as a tissue, but more as a 'mere' coexistence, a series of relationships between objects that almost never articulate in visual of formal ways, no longer 'caught' in architectural connections ... But if you have come to the insight that connection in no longer necessary, in a way you put a bomb at the base of your professional existence. If planning is not necessary, or is irrelevant ... why 'plan'? *(Rem Koolhaas)* ↗The term 'planning' appears 44 times in this book, ↗*Master Plan*, ↗*Analysis*

Plotter / Plat **1.** A plotter (ˈplɒtə, from *plot* 'to draw'), is an output device that depicts function graphics, technical drawings, and other vector graphics on various materials. Plotters are among the few appliances that directly reproduce vector graphics without first converting them into raster graphics. *(w)* **2.** A plat (ˈplæt or ˈplɑːt) is in the U.S. a map, drawn to scale, showing the divisions of a piece of land. City, town, or village plats show subdivisions into blocks with streets and alleys. Further refinement often splits blocks into individual lots, usually for the purpose of selling the described lots; this has become known as subdivision. The creation of a plat map marks an important step in the process of incorporating a town or city. *(w)* ↗Studio E, ↗*Grid*

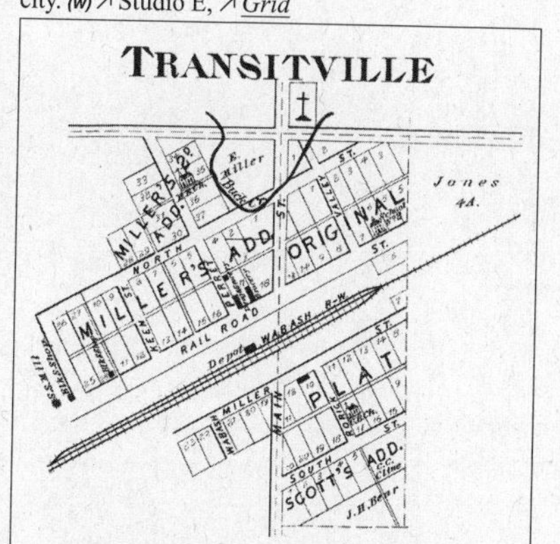

Plat: an 1878 map of Transitville in Tippecanoe County, Indiana

pool Architects ↗*Frei, Raphael*, ↗*Spoerri, Mischa*, ↗*Sonderegger, Andreas*

Post-Fordism Economic system that has developed since the 1970s. In contrast to the earlier Fordist model, Post-Fordism is characterized by a high level of flexibility in the areas of work organization, work groups, and task integration. The main maxim is the production system 'just in time' in which the amounts and the range of goods and services are determined by customer demand. This determines the 'miniaturization' of the firm in that every resource that is not used (e.g., superfluous storage space or production buildings), as well as labor forces or machinery, is eliminated.
↗ Identity Markers …

Private 'praɪvɪt, from the Latin *privatus* 'robbed' (from the masters); separated, standing for itself alone, not public, adjectival participle *privare* 'to rob', 'to free', 'to separate', also used as *privus* 'standing for itself', 'single'. *(dt)* ↗ Studio I, ↗ Complementary to *Public*

Public **1.** 'pʌblɪk, from Anglo-Norman *publik*, *public*, Middle French *public*, *publique* et al., and their source, Latin *pūblicus* 'pertaining to the people', alteration (probably after *pubes* 'adult men') of *populicus*, from *populus* 'people'. **2.** In the sequential accessing of spaces on the continuum between private and public space, the issue is repeatedly how to create different degrees of privacy and of transitional spaces. Such 'degrees of publicness', as Christopher Alexander terms them, play an important role in the discussion of the city, as from this viewpoint the purely public or purely private space rarely exists. **3.** Public space: those areas of a public corporation (council, province, state) accessible to the public, for example traffic areas, parks, or also buildings maintained by such corporations. *(dt)* ↗ Studio D, I, ↗ *Community*, ↗ Complementary to *Private*

Q

Quaternio from the Latin *quaternion* and means 'a whole consisting of four units'. C. G. Jung demonstrates the principle of synchronicity in a quaternio, a pair of axes made up of two pairs of terms that diametrically augment each other and can thus be understood in a similar way to, for instance, the pair of terms wave/particle in the transition from classic physics to quantum theory. Jung does not deny that each of the occurrences involved forms part of its own causal chain. Consequently, synchronicity does not question the causality principle, but expands it in a linear way to the purely acausal opposite pole: in their development things relate to each other in terms of meaning and are 'arranged the way they are'. *(w)* ↗ Studio A, ↗ *Jung, C. G.*, ↗ *Synchronicity*

R

Red **1.** red, the word red comes from the Old English *rēd*. In Sanskrit, the word rudhira means 'red' or 'blood'. In the Akkadian language of Ancient Mesopotamia and in the modern Inuit language of Eskimos, the word for red is the same word as 'like blood'. The words for 'colored' in Latin *coloratus* also mean 'red'. In Russian the word for red *krasniy*, comes from the same Old Slavic root as the words for 'beautiful' and 'excellent'. Red is next to orange at the end of the visible spectrum of light, and is commonly associated with danger, sacrifice, passion, fire, beauty, blood, anger, socialism, and communism, and also, in China and many other cultures, with happiness. *(w)* **2.** In the lecture by Marc Angélil red stands for built matter. ↗ 1m2/sec 08/15, ↗ *Black*, ↗ *Green*

Rein-Cano, Martin Martin Rein-Cano, who was born in 1967 in Buenos Aires. He studied History of Art at Frankfurt University and Landscape Architecture at the Technical University in Hannover and Karlsruhe. He obtained his first professional experience in the office of Peter Walker and Martha Schwartz in San Francisco. The *TOPOTEK 1* office was established in 1996. Martin Rein-Cano has given lectures at various universities and other cultural institutions worldwide and is regularly involved as a jury member in national and international competitions. ↗ ⊠, ↗ Studio I, ↗ *Lecturer*

Martin Rein-Cano

Responsibility **1.** rɪˌspɒnsə'bɪlɪti, from the Latin *responses*; *a)* the state of being responsible, accountable, or answerable ('responsibility is a heavy burden'), *b)* a duty, obligation, or liability for which someone is held accountable. *(w)* **2.** *Christopher Alexander:* We do not believe that these large patterns, which give so much structure to a town or of a neighborhood, can be created by centralized authority, or by laws, or by master plans. Instead we believe that they can emerge gradually and organically, almost of their own accord, if every act of buildings large or small, takes on the responsibility for gradually shaping its small corner of the world to make these larger patterns appear there. *(A Pattern Language)* ↗ Résumé …, ↗ *Incremental Urbanism*

Restaurant Krokodil Restaurant in which the Krokodil Group was founded. Address: Hohlstrasse 44, 8004 Zurich, Tel. +41 44 242 46 69. Opening hours: Mon. to Fri. 10 am–2.30 pm, 6 pm–12.30 am, Sat. 6 pm–12.30 am, Sun. closed. Recommended dish: paella. ↗ ⊠, ↗ *Architects Group Krokodil*, ↗ *Paella*

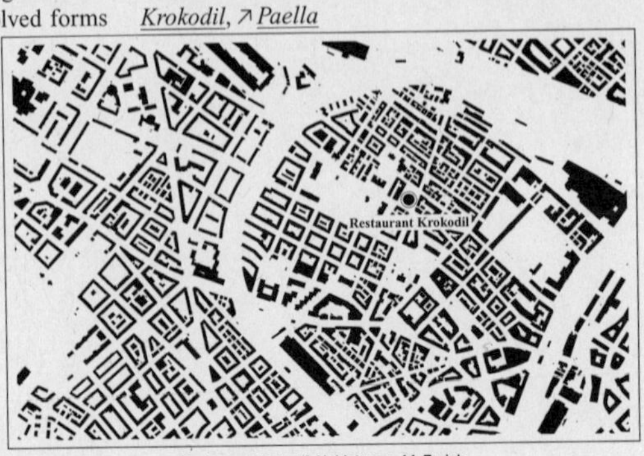

Restaurant Krokodil, Hohlstrasse 44, Zurich

Roth, Christopher Christopher Roth, who was born in 1964, is a cutter, director, scriptwriter, and film producer. His film *Baader* was awarded the Alfred Bauer prize. He undertook research with Georg Diez titled *80*81* and had a solo exhibition at *Esther Schipper* in Berlin. He was visiting professor at the Academy of Fine Arts, Nuremberg. ↗ ⊠, ↗ Studio A, ↗ *Lecturer*

Christopher Roth

Ruby, Andreas Andreas Ruby, who was born in 1966, is an architectural theorist and curator. From 1999 to 2001 he was editor of the architecture magazine *Daidalos*. Since 2001, with his partner Ilka Ruby, he has been leading *textbild*, an office for architectural communication. In 2008 they founded their own publishing house *Ruby Press* and launched their first title *Urban Transformation*. Andreas Ruby has taught at Kassel University, Cornell University Ithaca/NY, Ecole Polytechnique Féderale Lausanne, and the Metropolis Master Program Barcelona. ↗ ⊠, ↗ Just Imagine a City Is Made …, ↗ *Lecturer*

Andreas Ruby

run-of-the-mill (08/15) 'rʌn əv ðə mɪl; 08/15 (in English best translated by 'run-of-the-mill') is a term used in German for something entirely ordinary, in no way special, average, mediocre, made without great care, or something not worth mentioning. It can also be simply translated as 'standard'. There are three different explanations of the origins of this term. All of them are related to a type of machine gun, the MG 08/15, which was used during World War I. *(w)* ↗ ⊠, ↗ 1m2/sec 08/15

MG 08/15

S

Sausage 'sɒsɪdʒ; sausage is cooked or smoked meat processed by the butcher that also contains fatty tissue and, depending on the type of sausage, offal. Sausage meat is filled into tins or casings, which can be artificial or natural, the latter are made from intestines. According to how they are manufactured, sausages can be divided into three categories: Brühwurst (boiled), Kochwurst (cooked), and Dauerwurst (cured). *(w)* ↗ ⊠, ↗ *Barbecue*

Three types of sausages: boiled, cooked, and cured

Scales of Water Originally, the Glatt (*River Glatt*) occupied a far larger area of the Glatttal. The meandering branches of the river gradually disappeared into conduits. Christophe Girot and Lukas Schweingruber defined the original figure of the river as the spine of the Glatttal from which they conceived their studio work 'Scales of Water'. ↗ Studio J, ↗ *Landscape*

Schaefer, Markus Markus Schaefer, who was born in 1969, has a Master of Architecture from Harvard University, as well as a Masters in Neurobiology from the University of Zurich. He is a partner

Markus Schaefer

at *Hosoya Schaefer Architects* in Zurich, which he founded with Hiromi Hosoya in 2003. The firm has a wide spectrum of activities from interiors and entire buildings to urban design and research, such as a regional strategic study 'Metrobild' prepared for the Metropolitan region of Zurich, which resulted in a series of urban planning projects in the same area. Prior to founding *Hosoya Schaefer*, Markus Schaefer was a director of *AMO* in Rotterdam, the think tank and research department of *OMA*. ↗⊠, ↗Résumé ...

Schweingruber Zulauf Landscape Architects ↗*Schweingruber, Lukas*

Schweingruber, Lukas Lukas Schweingruber, who was born in 1964, studied landscape architecture at a HTL. He co-founded *Schweingruber Zulauf landscape architects* in 2005 together with Rainer Zulauf. For *Schweingruber Zulauf*, landscape architecture provides a field of experimentation within which the concepts of nature and landscape spaces can be studied. *Schweingruber Zulauf* work on city and landscape spaces at a wide range of scales. Amongst many others, the projects completed by *Schweingruber Zulauf* landscape architects include the design of the 'Oerliker Park' in Zurich-Oerlikon. ↗⊠, ↗Studio J, ↗*Architects Group Krokodil*, ↗*Schweingruber Zulauf Landscape Architects*

Lukas Schweingruber

Schwerzenbach *Municipality type:* workplace community, *region:* Glatttal, *district:* Uster, *post code:* 8603, *official municipality key:* 197, *population:* 4,527, *population density (intabitants/km2):* 1,701.9, *height above sea level:* 443 m, *area (ha):* 266. From August 1, 2012, following the completion of the new housing development 'Im Vieri', Schwerzenbach gained 488 new residents in a single go. *(st)* ↗*Glatt–the City*

Software **1.** 'sɒftweə; can be described 'easily changeable components', complementary to 'hardware', which represents the physical components. Generic term for all immaterial computer components that enable the computer to function by means of programs. In particular, software is used to carry out tasks in that it is evaluated by a processor and thus influences the work of software-directed appliances. *(w)* **2.** How can software be understood as an analogy of ideology? Ideologies serve the development and examination of socio-political action. They work programmatically and, like software itself, they are immaterial. They form a system of ideas, concepts, values, and standards. Ideology is a superstructure, a principle that guides actions, in much the same way that software functions invisibly in the background as program that instructs or directs actions.
↗Book chapter Software, ↗Studio A, E

Sonderegger, Andreas Andreas Sonderegger, who was born in 1965, studied architecture from 1985–1992 at ETH Zurich and carried out additional studies on high-rise construction from 1994–1995 at IIT Chicago. He has been a partner in *pool Architects* since 1998. *pool Architects* arose out of a discussion forum that brought together young practitioners in the field of urban planning. The office has won numerous competitions. They have realized a wide range of projects, from residential construction, school and office buildings to urban development. *pool Architects* taught as visiting professors at ETH Zurich.
↗⊠, ↗*Architects Group Krokodil*, ↗*pool Architects*

Andreas Sonderegger

Spoerri, Mischa Mischa Spoerri, who was born in 1964, studied architecture at ETH Zurich from 1985–1992. He became a partner at *pool Architects* in 1998. *pool Architects* arose out of a discussion forum that brought together young practitioners in the field of urban planning. The office has won numerous competitions. They have realized a wide range of projects, from residential construction, school and office buildings to urban development. *pool Architects* taught as visiting professors at ETH Zurich. ↗⊠, ↗*Architects Group Krokodil*, ↗*pool Architects*

Mischa Spoerri

Student **1.** 'stju:dnt, from Latin *studere* 'to work scientifically', 'to work diligently', in Middle High German 'one who learns'; describes a person who has enrolled for the purpose of study at a university, a university of applied sciences, or (in Switzerland) a technical college. To enroll at a third level institution, a secondary school leaving certificate (ability to study), of which there are various kinds, is required. The legal status of the student ends with ex-matriculation. **2.** 104 students took part in the Summer Academy. *(b30)* ↗⊠

Summer Academy students

Styrofoam 'staɪrəˌfom; Styrofoam is a transparent, foamed, white, amorphous, or partly crystalline thermoplastic. Amorphous Styrofoam is a widespread plastic used in many different areas of daily lafe. Styrofoam is used either as a thermoplastically processed material or as a foam (expanded polystyrene). The common trade names for polystyrene foam include Styropor, Styrodur (Germany), Austrotherm (Austria), Sagex (Switzerland), Hungarocell (Hungary), Floormate, Jackodur, Lustron, Roofmate, Styrofoam (USA), Telgopor (Spanish-speaking countries), and Frigolit (BASF). ↗⊠

Styrofoam model by Studio G

Styrofoam model by Studio D

Suburb 'sʌbɜ:b; a place on the edge of a larger city, either incorporated or independent. *(b15)* **2.** The suburb is an obsolete and contradictory form of human settlement. Many people want to live in the country; and they also want to be close to a large city. But it is geometrically impossible to have thousands of small farms within a few minutes of a major city center. *(Christopher Alexander, A Pattern Language)* **3.** Suburbia is, perhaps, almost okay. *(Preface by the Architects Group Krokodil)* ↗Preface, ↗*Periphery*, ↗*Suburbanization*

Suburbanization 'sʌbɜ:bənə'zeɪʃən; describes one of the fundamental urban development processes in industrialized countries in the 20th century, the large-scale and long-term de-concentration of urban regions, the spread of urban settlement patterns and population, work places, and infrastructure facilities into surrounding, previously rural, regions. Migration from the large cities has led to the suburbanization of rural communities, to the spread of new, generally less-dense developments on the periphery of urban regions, and to the development of satellite towns, which, however, rarely have a greater weight than the core city but continue to be oriented towards the latter in terms of their functional, economic, and social relationships. An important social factor of suburbanization is the emergence of the single family house in a 'green' setting as the dominant form of housing for the middle classes. *(b30)* ↗*Suburb*, ↗*Urban Sprawl*

Synchronicity ˌsɪŋkrə'nɪsəti; describes an inner experience (a vivid, exciting idea, a dream, a vision, or an emotion) and an external physical experience, which represents a (physically) manifested reflection of an inner (spiritual/psychological) state or its equivalent. In order to define this double occurrence as synchronicity, the inner experience must happen either chronologically before or

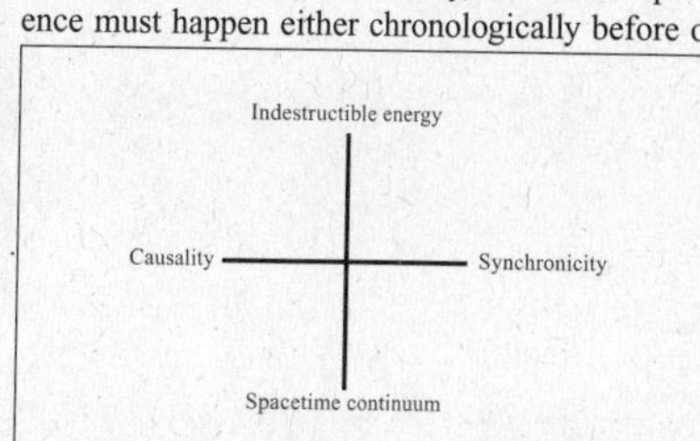

Synchronicity and causality juxtaposed in a quaternio

at exactly the same time as the external occurrence. Otherwise it could be assumed that the inner phenomenon is a reaction to the earlier, externally registered occurrence (which would make a causal explanation plausible). C. G. Jung used this term to describe both the phenomenon and the principle that lies behind it. *(w)* ↗⊠, ↗Studio A, ↗*Jung, C. G.*

July 2012 / August 2012

	23 Mon	24 Tue	25 Wed	26 Thu	27 Fri	28 Sat	29 Sun	30 Mon	31 Tue	01 Wed	02 Thu	03 Fri	04 Sat	05 Sun
Topic	Glatttal 6 x 15	City Building Blocks	Incremental Urbanism	Urban Landscapes	Design Studios	Interim Reviews	Excursion	Archipelago Collage City	Informal Urbanism	Diversity or Monotony	Hardware vs. Software	Design Studios	Final Reviews	Farewell
am	08.00 **Welcome** Introduction	08.00 **Design Studios** Workshop	08.00 **Design Studios** Workshop	08.00 **Design Studios** Workshop	08.00 **Design Studios** Workshop	09.00 **Design Studios** Presentations	09.00 **Bus Tour**	08.00 **Design Studios** Workshop	08.00 **Design Studios** Workshop	08.00 **Design Studios** Workshop	08.00 **Design Studios** Workshop	08.00 **Design Studios** Workshop	09.00 **Design Studios** Presentations	·Departure
pm	12.00 **Excursion** Visiting Glatttal						·Leutschenbach School ·Heerenschürli Sports Facility ·Hirzenbach School ·Aspholz Nord, Klee Residential development ·Viaduct Arches Lunch Break ·Josefswiese Lecture ·*Urban Transformation Zurich West* Walking tour ·Zurich West		12.00 **Lunch Lecture** ·Ulrich Görlich ·Meret Wandeler					
	06.30 **Presentations** ·HSLU Luzern ·BFH Bern Burgdorf ·FHNW Muttenz ·ZHAW Winterthur ·HSR Rapperswil	06.30 **Lectures** ·Freek Persyn 07.15 ·Emanuel Christ ·Christoph Gantenbein	06.30 **Panel** Moderation: ·Angelus Eisinger Lecture: ·Alexandre Chemetoff Discussion: ·Roger Diener ·Martin Heller ·Marcel Meili	06.30 **Lectures** ·Marc Angélil 07.15 ·Christophe Girot 08.00 ·Martin Rein-Cano	·No public programm			06.30 **Lectures** ·Andreas Ruby 07.15 ·André Bideau 08.00 ·Mark Lee	06.30 **Lectures** ·Alfredo Brillembourg ·Hubert Klumpner 07.15 ·Kunlé Adeyemi	06.30 **Lectures** ·Anne-Julchen Bernhardt ·Jörg Leeser 07.15 ·Boštjan Vuga 08.00 ·Don Murphy Swiss National Holiday	06.30 **Lectures** ·Jan Edler 07.15 ·David Trottin 08.00 ·Arno Brandlhuber ·Christopher Roth ·Sam Chermayeff	·No public programm	**Résumé** ·Markus Schaefer **Farewell** Apéro and Farewell-party	

Timetable of the International Summer Academy Zurich

T

Tabula Rasa 1. From the Latin 'smoothened writing tablet or slate', originally referred to a smoothened wax tablet and actually means a blank slate (also unknown quantity, blank paper). The modern idea of this theory is generally attributed to John Locke's expression of it in the 17th century. In his philosophy, *tabula rasa* was the theory that the human mind is at birth a 'blank slate' without rules for processing data, and that data is added and rules for processing are formed solely by one's sensory experiences. **2.** With regard to urban planning, this term means viewing the territory to be planned as an empty area (or as a blank paper), without incorporating what previously existed there.
↗ *Master Plan*, ↗ Complementary to *Incremental Urbanism*

Timetable 'taɪmˌteɪbḷ; timetable (plural timetables), a structured schedule of events with the times at which they occur, especially times of arrival and departure. *(w)* ↗ ⊠

Trottin, David David Trottin, who was born in 1965, is co-founder of *Périphériques Architects*, a Paris-based office. Since 1997, *Périphériques* has been a structure in constant evolution, exploring production and diffusion of architecture while proposing the negotiation and sharing of ideas between several partners as a platform for creation. *Périphériques* focuses on the fields of architecture and urbanism. The projects by *Périphériques* range from small-scale buildings to cultural and programmatically large and complex buildings. ↗ ⊠, ↗ Studio H, ↗ *Lecturer*

David Trottin

Typology Transfer taɪ'pɒlədʒi 'trænsfɜː; a method postulated by Emanuel Christ and Christoph Gantenbein, which is based on the assumption that there is no typological and architectural model for the city of today. As a rule, urbanist innovation stops shortly before the building. This is where their design concept starts: a typological model is transferred to a non-urban place in Zurich. From this confrontation a scenario for urban building develops. This scenario leads to a new architectural project that is expressed in plans and sections. Finally, the building volume and spaces of the interior are depicted in black and white photographs of large models. That is how a typological transfer works. *(Taken from: Christ / Gantenbein, Review N°II: Typology.)* ↗ Typology Transfer, ↗ *Building Typologies*, ↗ *Christ, Emanuel*, ↗ *Gantenbein, Christoph*

U

Ungers, Oswald Mathias Ungers was among the most important representatives of postmodernism in Germany. Urban analyses of the 'city in the city', urban organizational systems (e.g., Green Urban Archipelago for Berlin), and studies on the transformation of building volumes derived from geometric operations and regrouped to form exciting heterogeneous ensembles, as well as radical attempts at typologization form the core of his extensive and highly diverse work. Born in the Eifel in 1926, he died in 2007 in Cologne (both Germany), Ungers studied architecture in Karlsruhe and from 1950 worked in his own office in Cologne. Ungers taught at the TH Berlin and at Cornell University, Ithaca / NY. Among his best known buildings are the *Deutsches Architekturmuseum* in Frankfurt am Main, the new *Messehalle* on the Messegelände in Frankfurt am Main, and the new building for the *Wallraf-Richartz-Museum* in Cologne. *(la/la20)*
↗ Identity Markers …, ↗ Studio G, ↗ *Archipelago*, ↗ *Island Subcities*, ↗ *Morphology*

Universities of Applied Sciences 1. ˌjuːnɪ'vɜːsɪtɪz əv ə'plaɪd 'saɪənsɪz; a 'Fachhochschule' (FH) or 'University of Applied Sciences' (UAS) is a type of tertiary education institution found in German-speaking countries, sometimes specialized in certain topical areas. *(w)* **2.** The universities of applied sciences involved are: BHF Bern University of Applied Sciences, Bern (Barbara Neff, Bettina Neumann); FHNW University of Applied Sciences and Arts Northwestern Switzerland, Basel (Reto Pfenninger); HSLU Lucerne University of Applied Sciences and Arts, Lucerne (Reto Pedrocchi); HSR Technical University of Applied Sciences, Rapperswil (Andrea Cejka); ZHAW Zurich University of Applied Sciences, Winterthur (Thomas Schregenberger, Dominique Lorenz, Detlef Schulz (Bachelor); Urs Primas, Stefan Kurath (Master). **3.** The main concept was to take the major idea from the Krokodil master plan and to design urban space at the given areas. The students undertook a critical examination of the vision 'Glatt—the City' and developed their own projects in the Glatttal. **4.** *Glatt! Projekte für eine Stadt im Werden* (Glatt! Projects for a City in Progress). This book presents projects for the Glatttal by the universities of applied sciences involved. Each university is allotted its own chapter in which the research work, concepts and visualizations are shown along with introductory texts and a selection of the material produced. *Year of publication: 2013, 19 x 26 cm, ca. 256 pages, ISBN 978-3-906027-21-0.*

Urban-Think Tank (U-TT)
↗ *Brillembourg, Alfredo*, ↗ *Klumpner, Hubert*

Urban Sprawl 1. 'ɜːbən sprɔːl (noun, no plural); an unplanned, disorganized growth of housing, etc., on the edge of a city. **2.** The erection of buildings outside places that have developed coherently, or the uncontrolled and unstructured growth of places into the surrounding undeveloped space. The growth of settlement areas into the landscape. Urban sprawl is an aspect of suburbanization. In the context of the national research program 'Nachhaltige Siedlungs- und Infrastrukturentwicklung' researchers from Switzerland defined sprawl as follows: urban sprawl is a phenomenon that is visually perceptible in the landscape. The greater the surface area built upon, the more scattered the settlement areas, and the less intensive their use for residential or work-related purposes, the greater the amount of urban sprawl in the landscape. In this way quantifiable criteria of size, dispersion, and use of settlement areas augment the intuitive assessment of urban sprawl. *(w)* ↗ *Glatttal*, ↗ *Landscape*, ↗ *Suburbanization*

Uster *Municipality type:* workplace community, *region:* Glatttal, *district:* Uster, *post code:* 8610, *official municipality key:* 198, *population:* 32,547, *population density (inhabitants/km2):* 1,140.4, *height above sea level:* 464 m, *area (ha):* 2,854. In 2001 the town of Uster was awarded the Wakker Prize of the Swiss Heritage Society (SHS) for its urban and land use planning. (st) ↗ *Glatt—the City*

V

Volketswil *Municipality type:* work place community, *region:* Glatttal, *district:* Uster, *post code:* 8604, *official municipality key:* 199, *population:* 1,7572, *population density (inhabitants/km2):* 1,254.2, *height above sea level:* 475 m, *area (ha):* 1,401. The Volketswiler Gewerbemesse (VOGA, a trade fair) takes place every three years. Various businesses from the surrounding area are represented at this event. (st) ↗ *Glatt—the City*

Vuga, Boštjan Boštjan Vuga, who was born in 1966, graduated from the Faculty of Architecture in Ljubljana in 1992 and undertook postgraduate studies at the AA School of Architecture in London from 1993 to 1995. In 1996, together with Jurij Sadar, he founded *Sadar + Vuga* in Ljubljana. He is currently a guest professor at Adip, TU Berlin. As a guest editor, he took part in two issues of AB architectural bulletin. Boštjan Vuga has published numerous articles on current developments in architecture and urban planning. ↗ ⊠, ↗ Studio C, ↗ *Lecturer*

Boštjan Vuga

W

Walled City wɔːld ˈsɪti; cities with characteristic city walls developed in the early modern age. A number have survived to the present day and form part of the appearance of many towns in Europe. These little cities are grouped around palaces and castles whose fortifications separate them from their surroundings and protect them against external threats. Walled cities are very dense, concentrated, and functioned—at least until some time ago—as autonomous small biotopes, as islands in the landscape. For example, the French walled town of Neuf-Brisach. It was built at the beginning of the 18th century as a planned town in the shape of an octagon with a central parade ground and a checker-board pattern of streets and represents the ideal form of a fortified town. Under Louis XIV many similar fortified towns were erected along the French borders. (e/w) ↗ ⊠, ↗ Studio H, ↗ *Autonomous Urbanism*

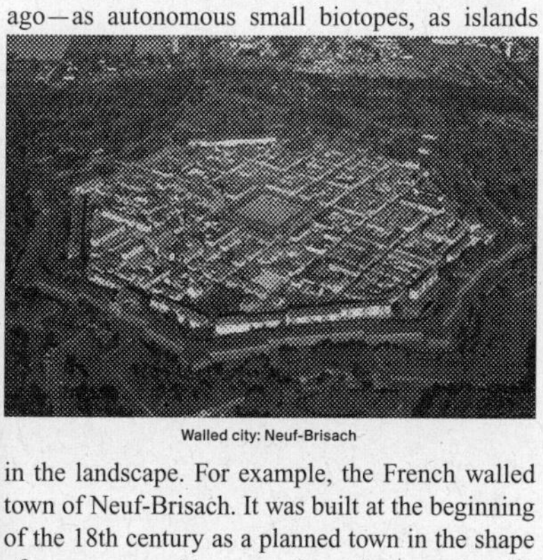
Walled city: Neuf-Brisach

Wallisellen *Municipality type:* workplace municipality, *region:* Glatttal, *district:* Bülach, *post code:* 8304, *official municipality key:* 69, *population:* 14,028, *population density (inhabitants/km2):* 2,171.5, *height above sea level:* 431 m, *area (ha):* 646. (st) Nowadays the native German-speaking populace speaks a mixture of Swiss German dialects. A standardized Zurich German with a tendency to integrate elements from standard language is widespread. Today one can recognize the natives of Wallisellen only from the way they pronounce the name of the municipality with a sharp 's'. ↗ *Glatt—the City*

Wandeler, Meret ↗ Schlieren, ↗ *Lecturer*, ↗ *Long-Term Photographic Observation ...*

Wangen-Brüttisellen *Municipality type:* work place municipality, *region:* Glatttal, *district:* Uster, *post code:* 8603, *official municipality key:* 200, *population:* 7,588, *population density (inhabitants/km2):* 959.3, *height above sea level:* 450m, *area (ha):* 791. (st) The municipality Wangen-Brüttisellen is the home of the Glatttal carrier pigeon breeding association. Flight competitions are held from mid-May to the end of August. ↗ *Glatt—the City*

Weather ˈweðər; from July 23, predominantly high-pressure weather with plenty of sunshine gradually established itself in Switzerland. Initially it was still cool due to the Bise wind. Subsequently the temperature increased noticeably. July 27 was, in many places, the hottest day of the year. The heat was followed by thunderstorms, many of them very heavy. The temperature sank dramatically and in many places reached no more than 20 degrees celsius. The month of August began with mid-summer weather and in most regions was sunny. The highest temperatures were reached on the national holiday when 28 to 32 degrees were recorded in low lying areas. A cloudburst at the end of the day interrupted the celebrations. The first half of August was not remarkable in weather terms. Sunny weather with summer temperatures predominated. (ms) ↗ ⊠

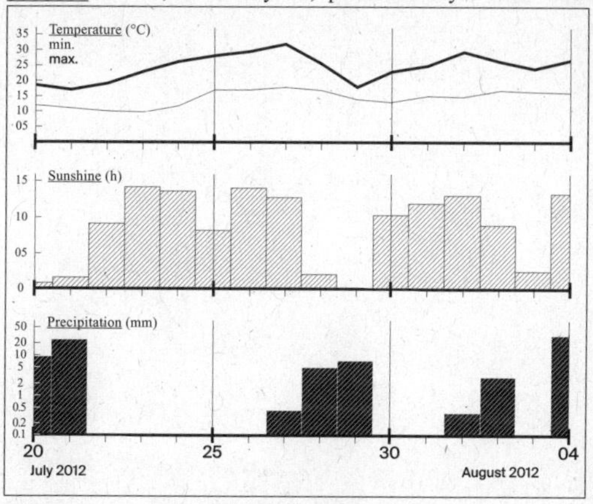

The weather from July 22nd to August 4th, 2012

X

↗ *Absence*

Y

↗ *Absence*

Z

Zierau, Frank Frank Zierau, who was born in 1961, founded his own office in Zurich in 1997 after working for *Meili, Peter Architects* from 1991 to 1995. Since then he has completed numerous projects at a wide range of different scales. His portfolio includes urban studies as well as projects for public, cultural, and private building types. Since 2011 he has been assistant professor at Zurich University of Applied Sciences in Winterthur (ZHAW). Frank Zierau was a lecturer at the Institute for Architecture and Planning of the University of Liechtenstein, Vaduz. ↗ ⊠, ↗ *Architects Group Krokodil*

Frank Zierau

Zwischenstadt ˈtsvɪʃən ʃtat; the term 'Zwischenstadt' was introduced by Thomas Sieverts and describes the partial peripheral dissolution of compact, historically developed European cities to create a new kind of urban form, a complex blend of town and landscape. This intermediate area, the urbanized landscape, is characterized by phenomena such as individualization, globalization, and mobility needs, and forms new landscape types that are amorphous, partly fragmented spaces embedded between commercial areas, wasteland, new residential developments, and traffic infrastructure. The areas bordering on the core city have developed into an almost accidental 'patchwork' of urban and landscape areas or bays. Increasingly they reveal functional, ecological, and aesthetic deficits. (ag) ↗ Identity Markers ..., ↗ Studio I, ↗ *Glatttal*, ↗ *Island Subcities*

Cross References:

↗ ⊠ (Figure)
↗ *Related contribution in the encyclopedia*
↗ Further information in contribution in the book

Sources:

(a) Wörterbuch der Architektur
(ag) Agglomeration Glatttal, http://culture-nature.com/agglomeration
(bk) Brockhaus, Die Bibliothek. Kunst und Kultur
(b15) Brockhaus in 15 Bänden
(b30) Brockhaus, Die Enzyklopädie in 30 Bänden
(d1) Duden, Das grosse Wörterbuch der deutschen Sprache in 10 Bänden
(ea) Encyclopedia of Aesthetics
(ec) Ed Cutler, http://architectureandurbanism.blogspot.ch
(h) Harenberg, Das Buch der 1000 Bücher
(k) Wörterbuch der Kunst
(la) Lexikon der Weltarchitektur
(la20) Lexikon der Architektur des 20. Jahrhunderts
(w) Wikipedia
(md) The metapolis dictionary of advanced architecture
(ms) MeteoSchweiz, Klimabulletin Juli / August 2012
(o) The Oxford Dictionary of Philosophy
(r) Bundesamt für Statistik, Bern, 1997
(st) Statistisches Amt Kanton Zürich, 2012
(u) Universal-Lexikon 2012

Picture Credits

Preface • *p. 5:* © Architects Group Krokodil • *p. 7:* © ETH Library Zurich, Image Archive of the Foundation *Luftbild Schweiz*, photo: Walter Mittelholzer • *pp. 8–9:* © Ralph Bensberg, Rainstrasse 86, 8143 Stallikon • *pp. 10–11:* © Architects Group Krokodil
Lectures • *p. 12:* © Succession Marcel Duchamp / 2012, ProLitteris, Zurich; © Jörg Müller • *p. 13:* © Jörg Müller; Maschinengewehr (source lost) • *p. 14:* © Jeff Wall Studio, The Bridge 1980, transparency in lightbox, 60.5 x 228.6 cm; © Marc Angélil • *p. 15:* © Benjamin Theiler; © Jesse LeCavalier • *p. 16:* © The Andy Warhol Foundation for the Visual Arts, Inc. / 2012, ProLitteris, Zurich; © berchtoldkrass space & options • *p. 17:* © Vittorio Magnago Lampugnani & Matthias Noell • *p. 18:* © Filip Dujardin • *p. 19:* © Studio Emanuel Christ & Christoph Gantenbein, ETH Zurich • *p. 20:* © Arnauld Duboys-Fresney pour Alexandre Chemetoff & associés • *p. 21:* © Andreas Ruby • *p. 22:* © Piotr Brzoza; © Keystone • *pp. 24–27:* © Ungers Archiv für Architekturwissenschaften UAA, Cologne; © Hilla Becher, 2012 • *p. 31:* © Ulrich Görlich and Meret Wandeler
Software • *p. 36:* source lost • *pp. 36–45 (Studio A, E):* © Architects Group Krokodil & D-ARCH, ETH Zurich • *p. 42:* from Oklahoma Historical Society, 1984; source lost
Networking • *pp. 50–59 (Studio D, F):* © Architects Group Krokodil & D-ARCH, ETH Zurich
Landscape • *pp. 64–79 (Studio I, J, B):* © Architects Group Krokodil & D-ARCH, ETH Zurich
Archipelago • *pp. 84–93 (Studio C, H, G):* © Architects Group Krokodil & D-ARCH, ETH Zurich • *p. 90:* © www.leuropevueduciel.com • *pp. 94–97:* from D-ARCH, ETH Zurich • *p. 94:* © John Hejduk's *Victims* from 1984, Johnston Marklee; Berlin as a Green Archipelago by Oswald Mathias Ungers in 1977 © Christian Seidel, Christian Rutherford and Gabriel Coin of the Technical University of Berlin
Résumé • *pp. 98–107:* © Architects Group Krokodil
Encyclopedia • *col. I:* © Caroline Vogel; from Kunlé Adeyemi; © Peter Fischli, David Weiss • *col. II:* © Marc Angélil • *col. III:* © UAA, Cologne; © Architects Group Krokodil • *col. IV:* © Architects Group Krokodil • *col. V:* © Architects Group Krokodil; from Jean-Jacques Benoît; Architects Group Krokodil • *col. VI:* from André Bideau; from Roger Boltshauser; from Arno Brandlhuber • *col. VII:* from Alfredo Brillembourg; from Alexandre Chemetoff • *col. VIII:* from Sam Chermayeff; © Mark Niedermann; © Cedric Price fonds, Collection Centre Canadien d'Architecture / Canadian Centre for Architecture, Montréal • *col. IX:* © Architects Group Krokodil • *col. X:* from Papyrus Ebers • *col. XI:* from G. Richter (nach Wermuth, 1953); from Roger Diener • *col. XII:* from Jan Edler; from Angelus Eisinger • *col. XIII:* © Architects Group Krokodil • *col. XIV:* from Rafael Frei; © Mark Niedermann; from Christophe Girot • *col. XV:* © Eno collection, Miriam and Ira D. Wallach Division of Art, Prints and Photographs, the New York Public Library, Astor, Lenox and Tilden Foundations • *col. XVI:* © Architects Group Krokodil • *col. XVII:* from Martin Heller; © Maurice Haas • *col. XVIII:* © FLC / 2012, ProLitteris, Zurich; from Hybrid Buildings, Pamphlet Architecture No. 11, New York, San Francisco, 1985 • *col. XIX:* © Architects Group Krokodil • *col. XXI:* from Hubert Klumpner • *col. XXII:* © Architects Group Krokodil • *col. XXIII:* © Peden + Munk; Architects Group Krokodil; © UAA, Cologne • *col. XXIV:* from Marcel Meili • *col. XXV:* © Maurice Haas; © Don Murphy; source lost • *col. XXVI:* © Maurice Haas • *col. XXVII:* D-ARCH, ETH Zurich; © Architects Group Krokodil • *col. XXVIII:* source: www.archimedespalimpsest.org © The British Library Board; ©Architects Group Krokodil • *col. XXIX:* © Architects Group Krokodil • *col. XXX:* from Freek Persyn; © from Kingman Brothers' Combination Atlas Map of Tippecanoe County, Indiana, reprinted by Tippecanoe County Historical Society / Lafayette Printing Company • *col. XXXII:* from Martin Rein-Cano; © Architects Group Krokodil • *col. XXXIII:* from Christopher Roth; from Andreas Ruby; from Imperial War Museum catalogue number Q 35445; © Caroline Vogel • *col. XXXIV:* from Markus Schaefer; from Lukas Schweingruber • *col. XXXV:* from Andreas Sonderegger; from Mischa Spoerri; © Architects Group Krokodil • *col. XXXVI:* © Architects Group Krokodil; © Architects Group Krokodil • *col. XXXVII:* © Architects Group Krokodil; from David Trottin • *col. XL:* © David Lotric; © www.leuropevueduciel.com • *col. XLI:* © Architects Group Krokodil • *col. XLII:* from Frank Zierau

Acknowledgments

Lecturers • Marc Angélil *(agps, Zurich / Los Angeles)* • André Bideau • Alexandre Chemetoff *(Alexandre Chemetoff & Associés, Bureau des paysages, Paris)* • Emanuel Christ *(Christ & Gantenbein, Basel)* • Roger Diener *(Diener & Diener Architects, Basel)* • Jan Edler *(realities:united, Berlin)* • Angelus Eisinger • Ulrich Görlich, Meret Wandeler *(ZHdK, Zurich)* • Martin Heller *(Heller Enterprises, Zurich* • Marcel Meili *(Meili, Peter Architects, Zurich)* • Freek Persyn *(51N4E, Brussels)* • Andreas Ruby *(textbild / Ruby Press, Berlin)* • Markus Schaefer *(Hosoya Schaefer Architects, Zurich)*
Studio Lecturers & Assistants • Kunlé Adeyemi *(NLÉ, Lagos, Amsterdam)* & Monica Velasco • Anne-Julchen Bernhardt, Jörg Leeser *(BeL Associates, Cologne)* • Arno Brandlhuber *(Brandlhuber+, Berlin)* • Christopher Roth *(Berlin)*, Sam Chermayeff *(June14 Meyer-Grohbrügge & Chermayeff, Berlin)* • Alfredo Brillembourg, Hubert Klumpner *(Urban-Think Tank, Caracas, São Paulo, New York, Zurich)* & Lea Ruefenacht • Christophe Girot *(Atelier Girot, Zurich)*, Lukas Schweingruber *(Schweingruber Zulauf Landscape Architects, Zurich)* & Dominik Bückers, Ilmar Hurxens, James Melsom • Mark Lee *(Johnston Marklee & Associates, Los Angeles)* & Sharon Johnston-Lee • Don Murphy *(VMX Architects, Amsterdam)* & Shaya Fallahi • Martin Rein-Cano *(TOPOTEK 1, Berlin)* & Anouk Kuitenbrouwer • David Trottin *(Périphériques Architects, Paris)* • Boštjan Vuga *(Sadar + Vuga, Ljubljana)* & Miha Čebulj
Universities of Applied Sciences • Barbara Neff, Bettina Neumann *(BHF Bern University of Applied Sciences, Bern)* • Reto Pedrocchi *(HSLU Lucerne University of Applied Sciences and Arts, Technology & Architecture)* • Reto Pfenninger, Dominique Salathé, Christina Schmacher *(FHNW University of Applied Sciences and Arts Northwestern Switzerland, Basel)* • Andrea Cejka, Catherine Blum *(HSR Technical University of Applied Sciences, Rapperswil)* • Thomas Schregenberger, Dominique Lorenz, Lorenzo Guliani, Detlef Schulz, Urs Primas, Stefan Kurath *(ZHAW Zurich University of Applied Sciences, Winterthur)*
Archives, Photographers & Authors • Ungers Archiv für Architekturwissenschaft *(Cologne)* • Die Photographische Sammlung / SK Stiftung, Kultur *(Cologne)* • Studio Jeff Wall *(Vancouver)* • ProLitteris, Schweizerische Urheberrechtsgesellschaft für Literatur und bildende Kunst, Genossenschaft *(Swiss Copyright Society for Literature and Fine Art)* • ETH Zurich, ETH Library, Image Archive • Peter Fischli *(Zurich)* • Jörg Müller *(Biel)* • Ralph Bensberg *(Stallikon)*
Special Thanks • Marc Angélil *(Former Head of Department of Architecture ETH Zurich)* • Patrick Gmür *(Director Office for Urbanism, Zurich)* • Sacha Menz *(Head of Department of Architecture ETH Zurich)* • Wilhelm Natrup *(Cantonal Planner and Head of the Spatial Planning and Surveying Agency Zurich)* • André Odermatt *(Zurich City Council)* • Pensimo Management AG • Martin Seiz *(Hamasil Foundation)* • Walter Ulmann *(Town Planner for the Town of Uster)*

Organisation
International Summer Academy Zurich

ETH Swiss Federal Institute of Technoloy Zurich, Department of Architecture & Architects Group Krokodil • Laura Blaufuss, Fabian Hörmann, Zeljko Medved *(Coordinators)* • Gabi Eisenreich, Heike Toussaint *(Assistants)* • Patrick Meng, Laura Pestalozzi, Raphael Jan Stähelin, Anouk Wetli *(Tutorial assistants)*

Sponsors

Blickpunkt Lebensraum ● Beat Odinga AG

Blickpunkt Lebensraum ● Stadtbauentwicklungs AG

SENNBPM AG

Info-Management Truninger Plot Scan Druck

ZUMTOBEL

• Basler & Hofmann AG • b+p baurealisation ag, • CCG Event-Technik AG • Mobimo Management AG • VBG Verkehrsbetriebe Glattal AG • Verein Zürcher Brockenhaus • Zumstein Büro- und Kunstmalbedarf

Project Partners

BSA Bund Schweizer Architekten
FAS Fédération des Architectes Suisses
FAS Federazione Architetti Svizzeri

BSLA

Schweizerische Eidgenossenschaft
Confédération suisse
Confederazione Svizzera
Confederaziun svizra
Swiss Confederation
Federal Office for Spatial Development ARE

sia
schweizerischer ingenieur- und architektenverein
société suisse des ingénieurs et des architectes
società svizzera degli ingegneri e degli architetti
swiss society of engineers and architects

uster
Wohnstadt am Wasser